FINDING *PEACE* WHEN YOUR LIFE IS *IN PIECES:*

THE PATHWAY BACK TO MEANINGFUL LIFE

Dr. Helen S. Peterson

Licensed Professional Counselor
Certified Grief and Bereavement Counselor

Copyright © 2015 by Dr. Helen S. Peterson
Licensed Professional Counselor
Certified Grief and Bereavement Counselor

Finding Peace When Your Life is in Pieces:
The Pathway Back to Meaningful Life
by Dr. Helen S. Peterson, Licensed Professional Counselor Certified Grief and Bereavement Counselor

Printed in the United States of America.

ISBN 9781498444675

All rights reserved solely by the author. The author guarantees all contents are original and do not infringe upon the legal rights of any other person or work. No part of this book may be reproduced in any form without the permission of the author. The views expressed in this book are not necessarily those of the publisher.

Unless otherwise indicated, Scripture quotations taken from the English Standard Version (ESV). Copyright © 2001 by Crossway, a publishing ministry of Good News Publishers. Used by permission. All rights reserved.

Scripture quotations taken from the King James Version (KJV) – *public domain.*

Scripture quotations taken from The Message (MSG). Copyright © 1993, 1994, 1995, 1996, 2000, 2001, 2002. Used by permission of NavPress Publishing Group. Used by permission. All rights reserved.

Scripture quotations taken from the New English Translation (NET Bible). Copyright ©1996-2006 by Biblical Studies Press, L.L.C. Used by permission. All rights reserved.

Scripture quotations taken from the Holy Bible, New International Version (NIV). Copyright © 1973, 1978, 1984, 2011 by Biblica, Inc.™. Used by permission. All rights reserved.

Scripture quotations taken from the New King James Version (NKJV). Copyright © 1982 by Thomas Nelson, Inc. Used by permission. All rights reserved.

Scripture quotations taken from the Revised Standard Version (RSV). Copyright © 1946, 1952, and 1971 the Division of Christian Education of the National Council of the Churches of Christ in the United States of America. Used by permission. All rights reserved.

Scripture quotations marked HCSB are taken from the Holman Christian Standard Bible®, Copyright © 1999, 2000, 2002, 2003, 2009 by Holman Bible Publishers. Used by permission. Holman Christian Standard Bible®, Holman CSB®, and HCSB® are federally registered trademarks of Holman Bible Publishers.Scripture quotations taken from the Good News Translation (GNT). Copyright © 1992 American Bible Society. Used by permission. All rights reserved.

www.xulonpress.com

Dedication

This book is dedicated to the memory of those whom I have loved and grieved: my dad, Gustave Peter Schultz; my brother, David Peter Schultz; my precious first husband, Robert Douglas Peterson; and my delightful second husband, Frank Hart, Sr., without whose lives and deaths I would have never understood the difficulty and joy of grieving. It is also dedicated to my precious son, Robert Scott Peterson, who willingly provides me with much love, wise advice, and good counsel as I continue on this marvelous journey in widowhood.

My beautiful and talented daughter-in-law, Angela, and my six wonderful grandchildren- Rebecca, Abigail, Samuel, Natalie, Andrew and Jon Luke- have helped me through some of the most difficult times of my life. Their child like enthusiasm has inspired me to maintain a positive and joyful outlook on life even when I have felt most alone. I am most grateful for the heart-warming lessons each one of my family members has taught me.

My dear friends – Betty Murphy, Marie King, Victoria Mitchell and Cynthia Ellison – have been constant sources of support. How grateful I am to have them in my life!

Endorsements

"I have had the privilege of knowing Helen for more than a decade. She is a true, selfless, biblical counselor of hurting hearts. As a pastor, it has blessed me to see her steadfastly minister God's healing truth to countless individuals, including myself. The book you hold in your hands does not come from some sterile academic environment, but from a professionally-trained counselor who has suffered deeply. During each of her losses, I saw Helen calmly keep her hope in the Lord, and live out her Christian faith in dark, lonely times that would have broken many. Hence, I encourage you to drink from the wisdom the Lord has imparted to her so that you might more readily face your own storms."

Rev. Charles S. Mitchell,
Pastor Midway Baptist Church,
Pine Mountain, GA

"This book by Dr. Peterson is a wonderful resource for those of us who are tasked with helping our patients and friends in their time of mourning after losing their husband or wife. I plan to purchase several copies to give to patients, family members, and friends when they are dealing with the death of the one they love the most."

David B. Roberts, MD

"No experiences of the loss of loved ones have compared to the loss of a wife of more than forty-two years of life together. I've certainly experienced confusion, anger, guilt, and hopelessness. I have learned that there are many losses along the path of life that result in our life falling into pieces. One of the most positive parts of this book is the way the reader is directed to the Holy Scriptures. I feel sure that the words, quotations and guidance from this book will be used by the Holy Spirit to guide and encourage many persons to face life from a different point of view."

James E. Rodgers, Sr.,
Businessman, former widower

"Dr. Peterson writes from her personal experiences of several losses in her life. She has been an example of one who has experienced weakness, strength, doubts and courage as she has walked the pathway of grief and mourning. Her understanding of the struggles and victories of widowhood are evident in her writing. It will be a source of great encouragement for all who lose loved ones."

Marie King, Businesswoman,
wife and friend

"Dr. Peterson provides insight into the challenges one experiences when faced with widowhood or similar loss. She also provides positive suggestions for making those experiences rich and meaningful. I believe it will be a resource filled with wisdom and comfort for many who suffer grief and bereavement after the death of their most loved one."

Ronald Lee,
Funeral Director

Preface

Human life is the essence of God's creativity. We are created in God's image, and within us we have the substance of His life. What that really means is not entirely clear to me. But, if we were created to be with Him, to glorify Him, and to be company for Him, then He certainly must have made us very much like Himself. Every parent or every creator creates out of his or her own essence. Therefore, life that God created out of the very essence of His being is very beautiful and very precious. It is the most joyful gift we could ever receive on this earth; conversely, the death of that precious life is the saddest loss we could ever endure.

Because of the imperfection, which came into this world and tainted life, living has limitations. Originally our human bodies were created to live forever just as our spirit lives forever. Because of the imperfection of sin that put a wedge between God and us, the immunity from disease and decay was lost on this earth. Therefore, we die of illnesses, accidents and the deterioration of our bodies. The death of our bodies is the consequence of the imperfection that entered this world after the miracle of creation.

When a loved one dies of disease, accident, or old age, we often forget that it was not meant to be that way in the beginning. Perhaps one of the reasons we don't think much about death while we are alive and healthy is because, in the original scheme of things, we were not supposed to die. Perhaps our denial may not be denial at all. Perhaps it is the way we are programmed in our soul or spirit.

Of course, we become preoccupied with loving those we have here on earth. We become attached to people and things and don't want to depart from them any sooner than we must. Those who do not know that they will live eternally with the Father in Heaven fear that death is the end of their existence. Those who believe and know in their spirit that they are an integral part of the Father's family may fear the experience of death because of the pain and the departure from the familiar. Nevertheless, they have within themselves the knowledge that they will live eternally with the Father and someday be reunited with those they love, if those, too, have accepted the gift of eternal life for the spirit. The fear of where they will exist beyond life is nonexistent.

Why then do those of us left behind when a loved one dies, grieve so deeply? It is not because we do not know the whereabouts of our loved ones. We know that those who have accepted the gift of eternal life provided by the sacrifice that Christ made are with the Heavenly Father forever. It is because we yearn for the familiar connections that made our lives meaningful. We miss the communication, whether spoken or unspoken, provided by that person "being." We often find, only in those times of grief, that life does not have its greatest value as humans "doing," but rather, as humans "being."

We miss the bonds of love, which have developed from being a part of the living experience of that other person. We miss the essence of that person's spirit and soul—all that made that person who she or he was. We often have depended upon that loved one for advice or encouragement. While God has told us to "bear one another's burdens," sometimes our loved ones have been too willing to bear our burdens. We have not grown up to use the gifts that God has provided us. Because our loved ones, too, have felt a need to be valuable, sometimes they have willingly helped us to live our lives. The expression of their love has become our very downfall. When they die and leave us, so often we have to learn to see ourselves as fully mature human beings. We have to look deep inside, where hopefully, we have stored God's truths, and where we have accumulated a wealth of experience to give us guidance. We often have to learn who we are apart from the loved one. While this seems difficult to do, we really begin to be who God wants us to be when we learn to function, using the talents and gifts with which He has provided us. This is a time we must become totally dependent upon Him to provide wisdom to use those abilities. As we turn our dependence on to Him, and as we seek His wisdom through His written word, we come to know Him, not only for *what* He has done in creating us, but also for *who* He is.

So often, when we grieve, it is as though we are stunned with the realization that living can be very painful. Much of the time we have lived as though in a fairy tale, not recognizing what it really means to live in this dark world. That loved one has been a buffer for us. When that comfort zone is removed, the exposure we experience is shocking, painful, and confusing. For a while we are bewildered. We suffer, not just the shock of losing that precious one in our life, but we also suffer the shock of having to face living more realistically. This experience affects both young and old. Youngsters suddenly become hesitant to do those things that they used to do so successfully. Adults falter in their decisions and goals while growth takes place and they regain balance. Children learn, with their simplistic faith, that God is their source of comfort. Adults learn this, even Christian adults, but often only after they try to hide the pain from themselves in an effort to be their own comforters.

As Christians it is so beneficial to spend time crying out to God and telling Him of the pain and confusion we are experiencing. Certainly, He already knows about it. He experienced such grief when He had to turn His face away from His Son and from the sin He carried to the cross. When we cry aloud to Him, we empty ourselves of the sadness of the moment. This has healing power. Once emptied, we can then go on for a time, in a state of peacefulness. Of course, we may have to do this many times until those tears perform the work of healing within us. God, in His understanding of what the human experience would be like, programmed us to be able to release those tears of anguish and to regain balance for the moment, as we achieve the greater balance in our living.

God knows that even when we come to Him time and time again with the same pain, it is a part of how He created us. As God, He does not forget His children. He loves us so deeply that when we err and stray, He also feels the pain over and over again. By being created in His image, we experience the pain repeatedly until the healing takes place. While sometimes we must permit ourselves to depend upon friends and loved ones to hold our feelings in their loving hands, the true value in grieving is to grow resilient and to able to be dependent upon the Great Comforter and Healer. Our friends, loved ones, and even outstanding professional counselors are wonderful to have. They are God's gifts to help us along the way. But, ultimately, we must grow by ourselves with our God, the God who really understands us, because He knows our every thought and every experience in life. He knows how He made us and what His ultimate purpose is for our lives. Our human counselors have knowledge of the grief experience and can help us to gain comfort, but they are limited by what we let them know about ourselves. Our Heavenly Father can be the only complete Counselor because only He knows us completely.

It is my hope that as you choose selections to read that are meaningful to your experience, you will develop a very positive outlook toward this very difficult experience in your life. May God grant you mercy as He heals you and grows you into a more wonderful human being.

Table of Contents

Introduction xv
    Widowhood: Is It an Ugly Word? xvi

Isolation 17
    When You Have to Grieve Alone 18
    Broken and Feeling Incapable of Facing Life Alone 20
    Feeling Empty, Numb, and Tired 22
    Feeling Shriveled and Spent 25
    Feeling Strange Attending a Social Event Alone 28
    Feeling That Your Loved One Is Forgotten 31

Loneliness 35
    When Loneliness Incapacitates You 38
    When All You Want Is That Old Relationship 41
    When Pining Overcomes You 43
    Moving beyond Yearning 45
    Looking for a New Relationship 47
    Needing to Feel Loved 49
    When You Think That God Has Deserted You 52
    When Your Days Weigh Heavily and Your Nights Are Worse 54
    When You Make Poor Choices because of Loneliness ... 56
    When Loneliness Can Be a Blessing 58

Pain 61
    You Detest the Pain and Suffering of Grief 62
    When the Pain Seems Too Hard to Bear 65
    Trying to Avoid the Pain of Grief 67
    When Time Has Passed and You Still Hurt Terribly 70
    Whammed by Grief Again 72
    When Words Hurt 75
    When Your Nightmares Will Not Cease 77
    When Nighttime Brings No Solace from the Pain 80
    Coping with the Anniversary Date 83
    When You Crave a Change 85

Confusion 87
    When Confusion Abounds 88
    When You Feel Really Mixed Up 90
    No Personal Time to Think 93
    Thanks for the Advice, but 95

    Living Life as a Caterpillar 97
    Life as a Patchwork Quilt 99
    Emotional Endoscopy 101
    Everything Has Changed 103
    Afraid You Are Losing Your Mind 106

Fear 109
    Fear—Friend or Foe? 110
    Afraid to Go On 112
    When Fear of the Future Robs Your Joy 114
    Wondering If Your Spouse Would Approve 116

Anger..119
    Why Did God Take My Loved One? 120
    Questioning the Love of Your Spouse 123
    When Acceptance Won't Come 125
    When You Are Very Angry 128
    Angry with God 131
    When Your Sorrow Makes You Bitter 134

Guilt 137
    When You Feel Guilty because You Feel Relieved 138
    When Guilt Won't Set You Free 141
    Could Haves and Should Haves 143
    When You Have Made a Major Mistake 145

Hopelessness 147
    When You Seem to Be Drifting through Life 148
    When You Feel as though Your Life Is on Hold 150
    When Healing Is Slow 153
    When You Feel Tied to the Past 155
    When You Feel as If Life Is Meaningless 157
    When You Begin to Feel Sorry for Yourself 159
    When the Future Seems So Bleak 161
    When One Day Runs into the Next 164
    When You Are Too Close to See 167
    When You Feel as though Your Time Is Wasted 169
    When You Have No Motivation 171
    When Times Are "Awful" and You Are Discouraged 173
    When You Wonder If God Really Has a Plan for You 176
    When Faith Is All You Have Left 178

Bibliography 181

INTRODUCTION

Whatever is true, whatever is noble, whatever is right, whatever is pure, whatever is *lovely,* whatever is admirable—if anything is excellent or praiseworthy-think about such things.

-Philippians 4:8 (NIV)

Widowhood: Is It an Ugly Word? . . .
Consider that which is lovely!

As widows and widowers sometimes we get ourselves stuck in feelings of sadness, regret, guilt, anger, loneliness, and self-pity. You might wonder how you could ever think there would be anything positive about widowhood. Well, this book was written just for you. You may be newly widowed, or you may be widowed for some time and wondering if life ever will bring fulfillment again. I have good news for you. It can and it will.

Since it is important to reframe things . . . to give them new meaning . . . let us begin with the terms *widow* or *widower*. These terms can be shunned, or they can be worn as a shining crown of precious jewels. I have chosen to think of widowhood as a shining crown, and I hope you will, too. While widowhood is often painful and lonely, it is a state to be honored and revered. It means that you have been loved deeply, and that in turn, you have loved deeply. It means that together you were able to weather the storms of life, for however long, and you made it "till death do us part." It means that your departed spouse does not have to suffer the pain of grief. It means that he or she fulfilled their work on earth and is now enjoying the presence of God. It means that our Heavenly Father rejoices that one more of His little children is now safely at home with Him. It means that God still has a purpose for *you* and that your work is not yet finished. And best of all, it means that God loves you so much that He wants you to grow in ways that you have never yet dreamed about—ways that will help your faith grow stronger and your life to become more of a channel of His love to others here on this earth.

At this point you may not believe all of the above could ever be true. I can testify to you that it can. I have been widowed twice and have survived. It is not an easy thing to do because you must change many of the ways that you think. And, you must be willing to relinquish your grief to the Master Healer.

Because it may be difficult to concentrate for long periods, this book is intended to be read in any order as the needs emerge. You may wish to read a part of one section and then move on to a part of another section. As you read, remember that God has said: *"'For I know the plans I have for you,' declares the Lord, 'plans to prosper you and not to harm you, plans to give you hope and a future'"* Jeremiah 29:11(NIV). God is faithful to His promises. He will be faithful to you.

ISOLATION

When You Have to Grieve Alone . . .
Consider that which is lovely!

The journey through grief after bereavement is often a lonely one. Once the activity of the funeral is over, it seems as though people go on with their lives and are not aware of the pain you are experiencing. Consequently, you begin to feel as though you must make it through this journey alone. You try the best you can to make your life go on, but sometimes you feel as though you are a failure because often you do not have focus or apparent direction. Unfortunately, the truth is that no one can complete your grief process for you. But another truth is that there is One who can make it more meaningful.

There is a story that is told about the great pianist Paderewski. On an occasion, a little boy got behind the curtains of the stage just before the concert was about to begin. Happily, he found the wonderful Steinway piano and made himself at home playing "Twinkle, Twinkle, Little Star." At that moment the curtains opened, and Paderewski entered the stage and crossed to the great piano. To the little boy, he said: "Don't quit. Keep playing." Soon he leaned over and with one hand he began to fill in the bass part. In a short while, his other arm reached over the youngster and began to play a wonderful obbligato. Together the youngster and the great master produced such music that it became the most remembered piece of the concert.

In your grief journey, you often make attempts to keep going on, but your efforts are hardly noteworthy. You feel bogged down and barely able to make each day count. The results often are inept, and you feel as though nothing you do is ever going to get you out of the pain you feel. However, with the hands of the Master around you, this part of your life can be truly beautiful. Your feeble attempts at revamping your life may seem simplistic and unimpressive. However, if you listen carefully, you may hear the Master saying to you: "Don't quit. Keep playing." As you depend upon His strength you will feel His arms around you and know that His hands are there, helping you turn your feeble attempts into true masterpieces.

Isn't it lovely to know that when you feel least capable, you become the most beautiful in God's sight? Isn't it wonderful to know that He turns your meager efforts into beautiful and meaningful experiences from which others, also, benefit?

When you feel that nothing you do is helping you or anybody else, Don't be a quitter. Keep on playing. The Master will make your efforts complete and beautiful. In time, you will play a new song.

"He put a new song in my mouth, a hymn of praise to our God. Many will see and fear and put their trust in the LORD."

-Psalm 40:3 (NIV)

"Pile your troubles on God's shoulders - he'll carry your load, he'll help you out. He'll never let good people topple into ruin."

-Psalm 55:22 (The Message)

Broken and Feeling Incapable of Facing Life Alone . . .
Consider that which is lovely!

    As a widowed person, sometimes you may feel as if you are just here, sort-of wandering through life without purpose or goals, incapable of facing life alone. An important part of your life has been wrenched away from you, and you feel broken. Your feelings are *genuine* but not necessarily *accurate.* During marriage, you became melded together, much like that which occurs when a welder joins one important piece of metal to another to make an entirely new and whole object. You often thought alike, enjoyed similar activities, and acted in ways that resembled your partner. You and your partner came to complement each other in such a manner that now, when the other part is gone, you feel broken and incapable of moving forward without someone in your life to love you and to help you. But, what joy to know that in spite of the many differences that were present when you started your journey together, the differences became fewer and the likenesses became greater. How wonderful to know that both of you learned from each other and, little by little, began to assimilate new qualities in your own unique way.

    While feeling isolated and incapable is unpleasant, those feelings will not last for long if you decide not to let them dominate your thoughts and actions. Sometimes you think that God sends people to be in your life forever. But, often He only sends them for a temporary time to help you fulfill your mission in life. Their influence can continue even while others come and help you move along the rest of the way. Because you were able to assimilate many of the characteristics of your partner that were essential for maintaining balance, *you* can now choose to strengthen those aspects that were good and lovely. Remember, you are more of a person now than you were when the two of you first began your journey together. You are more capable of facing life because the strengths of that loved one have now become some of your strengths. You may not realize it, because you "always" let your partner be dominant in some areas, but, you *have* learned and you *have* grown. Now, the secret to overcoming those feelings of incapability is to put that knowledge into practice, and soon you will gain a new perception of your own abilities to manage quite well. Believe that God has equipped you with what you will need to do a great job and you will.

> "If you give up when it's winter, you will miss the promise of your spring, the beauty of your summer, and the fulfillment of your fall.

If you do not give up, the peace of God can rule within you and you will sing with joy as you discover the new person within you who is emerging."

Helen S. Peterson

"I can do all things through Christ who strengthens me."

-Philippians 4:13 (NIV)

A Bird with a Broken Wing

I feel like a bird with a broken wing
Who's lost the desire to fly or to sing.
I feel I can do nothing but stay on the ground,
Depending on care from those all around.

The healing of wing and heart are long;
Life is bleak without my song.
Yet deep within there is a drive
To stir again and become alive.
One day my broken wing will heal,
And I'll awaken as I start to feel
The joy within of learning to thrive . . .
The wonder of practicing how to survive.

Until that time I will humbly pray
That God will help me through this day.
I'll yield myself to the wisdom above
And accept His plan with heartfelt love.

Helen S. Peterson

Feeling Empty, Numb, and Tired . . .
                          Consider that which is lovely!

There may be days when you feel completely empty and devoid of any real feeling. You are so tired that you don't want to do anything even though you know the work is staring you in the face. You wonder if these feelings are unusual. They are not unusual. They are a part of the grieving process that come and go until you have adapted to the loss in your life. Sometimes they happen even when you feel as though you have gotten a hold on things and that life is going to be okay again. But, generally, they happen when your physical resistance is low and you are tired. When they come, they seem to be so debilitating. The weather can be bright and sunshiny, and it seems that life should be cheerful and happy. But, for a short while, it isn't.

Sometimes you may just sit in a chair and do nothing, absolutely nothing. Other times you may try to get up and accomplish something, but often you find that is too boring, and you sit down again. You find you can't concentrate on any one thing, so nothing gets finished, which leaves you feeling even more frustrated. If you get into the car to go for a drive, you may wander aimlessly trying to assuage your grief by driving and driving and driving. It doesn't work because you always have to come back home. So, what are you going to do? How can you view this time of your life as a time that is lovely?

First, don't despair. These feelings are only temporary, and in time they will pass. Second, look for the littlest, tiniest thing to do that you can accomplish. It may be as simple as putting some dishes into the dishwasher or the sink. Congratulate yourself on your little accomplishment, and then try another easy task. Before you know it, you will be completing many little tasks that will enhance your sense of control in your life. It won't take away the emptiness, but it will help you to function better.

While you are busy getting some tiny tasks accomplished, talk out loud to your loved one. Of course, he or she can't hear you, but you can. Talking out loud to the one whom you miss will help you with the mourning process. That is different from grieving. Grieving is done inside of you, privately. Mourning is done outside of you, with others or with yourself by talking or writing or thinking out loud. No, you are not crazy. Grieving (within) and mourning (without) are essential parts of the process of healing. You must express yourself openly, but often your family and friends get tired of hearing you because they have already moved on. Expressing yourself out loud desensitizes you to the hurt and the pain that is inside. In time, it will help you to accept the permanency of the loss. So, consider it lovely to be able to express yourself aloud to or about the one you loved.

Consider it lovely that you were able to love enough to be hurt and "lost." If a person does not care, then they do not feel that pain. But, if you have allowed yourself to love and to be loved, then you have also allowed yourself to become vulnerable to the pain that comes with loss. It is wonderful to be loved. It is wonderful to love another. God did not originally intend that we should suffer that pain, but because He wanted us to know that He understands our pain, He allowed Himself also to suffer the loss of a loved one. Perhaps it is lovely to know that you can join with God through understanding suffering and pain. Perhaps it is also lovely to know that when you are past this difficult time in your life, you will be able to reach out to others to support them with real understanding as they, too, experience losses in their lives. Perhaps you will be a willing listener when others will not. What a blessing you will be.

"Blessed are those who mourn, for they will be comforted."
-Matthew 5:4 (NIV)

Why Did God Take My Loved One Away?

You are struggling with grief; your heart is filled with pain.
You wonder if true joy will ever come again.
The one you loved so dearly, to whom you gave your life
Has moved beyond the earth, with its toil and its strife.
You wrack your brain for things unsaid or things you might have done.
But within your heart, you know they'd say "We really had great fun!"
If you had what you wished, they'd be with you still.
But deep within your weary brain You try to believe it was the Father's will.
You question, and you ponder, ever wondering how or why.
Through the sadness and the tears, you wish it had been you to die.
Will your sorrow ever cease?
Will there ever be an end to the long and lonely dearth?
These questions we often ask when we struggle here on earth.
The answer lies in waiting while the work of grief is done.
But one bright morning you will see the shining sun.

Life will go on, though not quite the same;
And sometimes in anguish you'll whisper their name.
But gradually, gradually your life will revive.
You'll rejoice once again to still be alive.

Helen S. Peterson

Feeling Shriveled and Spent . . .
                              Consider that which is lovely!

    Did you know that humans can live for several minutes without oxygen, almost a month without water, and as much as six to eight weeks without food? But, as soon as they feel they are no longer loved their spirit begins to shrivel and die. Sometimes, after you have lost the one you love so dearly, you may feel as though you have become shriveled up inside and just about good for nothing anymore. The emptiness that comes when that person is no longer there to affirm you is sometimes so painful. You still have lots of love to give, but he or she is not there to receive it. And while you may believe that he or she loved you dearly, it is just so hard to make the memory of that love a present reality for yourself. The feeling that you no longer have an attachment to the one you have loved can be debilitating. It can cause you to give up on the goals and aspirations that once were yours. It can make you feel as though you just don't want to face the world, with all of the problems and challenges. It can make you want to curl up under a blanket in a dark room and sleep the rest of your life away without any feeling or any further interaction in life.
    Some folks do just that, and if that is what they choose to do, then there is little we can do to make them change. But, as they hide themselves from life, they become more and more sequestered and more and more shriveled, a little like a grape that is becoming a raisin but without the sweetness that we find in raisins. Further, they may think that withdrawing from life is the best way to cope. But inactivity simply makes the bones brittle, the joints ache, and the eyes stop smiling.
    The good news is this. We don't have to live that way. When you move out of your own little world and give love to others, no matter if you *feel* that love or not, it generally will be reciprocated. That is why so many widowed persons enjoy having a pet. They can give their pet all the love they want, and that pet will be receptive to it. So it is with humans. When God told us to love Him first and then to love others as we love ourselves, He didn't just mean it as a command to follow so we would not be selfish. He meant it for our spiritual and psychological good. He knew that in giving love to Him and to others we would once again regain that sense of attachment that has been lost, both to Him and to those around us. He knew that it is wise for us to move out of ourselves, out of our feelings of emptiness and loneliness and into the riches of giving and thereby receiving that gift that is so precious to all of us—the gift of knowing we are loved.

It is lovely to know that it is never too late to move out of our shriveled state and once again join the world. It is lovely also to know that what we have learned we can use to help others who may feel as though they have shriveled and died.

Stop sweating the small stuff. Don't worry about who doesn't love you, who has more, or who's doing what. Instead, cherish the relationships you have with those who love you. Think about how God *has* blessed you. And, choose, each day, to do things that promote mental, physical, spiritual, and emotional health.

"My lips will glorify You because Your faithful love is better than life."
-Psalm 63:3 (Holman Christian Standard Bible)

If I Had My Life to Live Over

If I had my life to live over, I would have talked less and listened more.

I would have invited friends over to dinner even if the carpet was stained and the sofa faded.

I would have eaten the popcorn in the 'good' living room and worried much less about the dirt when someone wanted to light a fire in the fireplace.

I would have taken the time to listen to my grandfather ramble about his youth.

I would never have insisted the car windows be rolled up on a summer day because my hair had just been teased and sprayed.

I would have burned the pink candle sculpted like a rose before it melted in storage.

I would have sat on the lawn with my children and not worried about grass stains.

I would have cried and laughed less while watching television—and more while watching life.

I would have shared more of the responsibility carried by my husband.

I would have gone to bed when I was sick instead of pretending the earth would go into a holding pattern if I weren't there for the day.

I would never have bought anything just because it was practical, wouldn't show soil or was guaranteed to last a lifetime.

Instead of wishing away nine months of pregnancy, I'd have cherished every moment and realized that the wonderment growing inside me was the only chance in life to assist God in a miracle.

When my kids kissed me impetuously, I would never have said, "Later. Now go get washed up for dinner."

There would have been more "I love you's"; More "I'm sorrys" . . .

But mostly, given another shot at life, I would seize every minute . . . look at it and really see it . . . live it . . . and never give it back.

Bombeck. December 2, 1944

Feeling Strange Attending a Social Event Alone . . .
Consider that which is lovely!

I received an invitation to attend a wedding of a dear young lady whom my spouse and I had known since her early teens. While I knew I wanted to be there, I also knew it would be painful to go by myself. Several hours before the appointed time, I almost convinced myself that I really didn't have to go. After all, there would be so many others there that they wouldn't miss one new widow who didn't feel comfortable being alone. But, I forced myself to get dressed and sadly drove myself to the church and later to the site of the reception. The first pain I faced was when the handsome young usher innocently asked me, "Are you alone?" The second moment of pain came when at the reception I had no idea where to sit. Everyone else seemed to be a "couple" and there I was, alone and without a spouse. At first, sorrow crept over me, and then fear of rejection quickly took its place. How could I do this alone after having my spouse with me for over forty-three years? I didn't want to be there. I would be much more comfortable curled up under the covers in bed, alone and away from all those who seemed to be so happy together. How does one change that painful experience into one that is lovely?

As I lived through each moment of my experience, I thought of how wonderful it was that I had forty-three years of unconditional love with the spouse I had lost. I considered that some people have many fewer years and some never have that blessing at all. I congratulated myself on having the courage to face that situation and to determine that I would not allow myself to be alone on such a happy occasion. As I did so, I found that my sense of humor became my ally, and I became the "hit" of the evening. Others were inspired by the fact that I openly asked them if I could become a "part of their family" for just a little while. Still others teased me about being "too happy" as a widow. The ladies were so glad to see me there, and the gentlemen were only too happy to get me food, drinks, and even escort me to my car after the celebration ended. I found, much to my surprise, that even though I was alone, I was not alone at all. I found that people whom I had hardly known were so kind and so accepting. And I found that the thoughts of rejection and loneliness that I had harbored before the event were certainly ill-founded. Instead of feeling alone and out of place, I felt loved and lovely.

It takes a lot of courage and often, great fortitude, to face social situations alone when you have been accustomed to being with your spouse. The lovely part of doing so is that you learn you have that courage and that fortitude. You find that the first time you do so, it may be a little uncomfortable, such as when you want to go out to dinner at a lovely restaurant but then you have to sit by yourself and pretend you are happy. It often feels awkward to join a group of married persons at a church gathering since you are no longer married. But, when you do so, you find that you are not rejected. The people who loved you before still love you now. They may unintentionally forget to invite you to gatherings because of your single status, but then you learn that when you ask to be included they are very happy that you did. Because of your single state, you learn to become more assertive. It is easier at first to allow yourself to be left out because you feel different. However, when your need to belong reasserts itself, you find a way to be a part of that which you had been at one time. In time, you also find ways to join others who enjoy your single state. Once you realize that there are many benefits to being single, you no longer feel awkward as you happily make a new "normal" life for yourself.

My Precious Spouse

When you gave me your love,
You gave me all of you.
All of you is too much for me to comprehend;
Overwhelming that my world was changed forever.
And because you loved me so,
I became wholly yours.
When you kissed my lips, you kissed my soul.
When you held me in your arms,
You took my very being into your heart.
When you looked into my eyes you knew
Everything there was to know about me.
You were my life, my breath, my being.
You helped me use my strength to grow.
I didn't realize how much I needed you.
Now you are gone,
And I am struggling to learn anew how to live.
You believed in me when you were here;
I must believe in me now that you are no longer here.
I *will* grow strong again
And make it through my ordained days.

Yet, I will never forget that you were the one who
Gave me love and life and hope and grace to grow.
I shall not disappoint you . . . no, my love, I will go on!

Helen S. Peterson

Feeling That Your Loved One Is Forgotten . . .
Consider that which is lovely!

Thanksgiving Day came and went. Harold had sadness such as he had not experienced for several months. He had gone through the day, Thanksgiving Day, that marked the eleventh month without his precious wife of forty-three years, and not one family member had called him. It was true that he was with his children and grandchildren, and they had been kind enough. But, his brothers and sisters had gone on with their lives, probably not even aware that he had great pain in his heart. He was hurt, angry, and sad. How could the life of his wonderful spouse be forgotten so easily? She had done so many meaningful things for them through the years, so why had his own siblings not remembered that he was experiencing pain that was so heavy and so severe?

These are the kinds of thoughts that often come to those who are living with sorrow. So much of it is because the wound is deep and the pain does come more intensely during the holiday season when "family" is paramount. It comes whenever you feel alone and without the concern of others whom you think should feel the pain as you do. It is hard to be patient with others. They do care, but often they don't understand the pain you feel because they have not experienced your loss. They may be so busy dealing with life itself that they cannot stop to think about death. It is only when you have gone down the bereavement path that you become truly aware of the suffering of others such as yourself. Even then, you, too, may become so busy with the process of existence that you overlook the struggles of others.

So, what is there that can possibly be considered *lovely* about this time in your life? At first glance it would seem that there is nothing lovely or good or valuable about this time. But, if you can change your thoughts for just a few moments, you can remember the wonderful things that used to be. You can appreciate that you had those times that many never have had. You can appreciate that you understand the meaning of love and the pain that the loss of love brings to you. You can realize that someday others will understand even though they do not at this time. You can decide to make it less painful for them in the future or to ignore their pain as you feel they have done yours. Of course, it is lovely if you choose to forgive and to give of yourself because you have learned from your pain. You also can learn to share the thoughts and feelings, in a loving manner, that bombard your mind and soul, and thereby, teach others to be more mindful of the pain that we all, at some time, will experience. Becoming more empathic is a great gift. It is a gift that draws people to you because they know you are real . . . authentic . . . in your understanding. Consider these things. Indeed, they are lovely.

"God has said, 'Never will I leave you; never will I forsake you.'"
-Hebrews 13:5 (NIV)

Remember Me

Remember me as the dawn
Breaks forth into glorious day,
And the pain of the long dark night
Slowly fades away.

Remember me when you see
One rose bud covered with dew.
Remember the countless times I said,
"Dear One, I truly love *you*."

And in the course of remembering
When you shed a few sad tears,
Remember how we dearly loved
For all those cherished years.

Remember that love will never stop
Though death has bid us part.
Ours was a true and precious love.
You satisfied my heart.

Though it made me sad to die
And leave you there with grief,
Rejoice, for now my pain is gone.
I have joy beyond belief.

Isolation

You must go on and do the work
That God has planned for you to do;
He will provide the joy you need,
He'll lead the way for you.

When in Heaven we meet again
I know that there will be
A million joyful tears to flow
Because you're here with me.

                    Helen. S. Peterson

Loneliness

When Loneliness Envelopes You Like a Shroud . . .
Consider that which is lovely!

Loneliness is so overwhelming. It is as if you are alone in this world with not a soul who cares about whether you are alive or not. It wrenches your heart and makes the hole that is there just a little bigger and more painful. At times when you experience loneliness, you must hold on to *hope*.

Hope is the light ahead through the darkness of this particular tunnel. It is the beacon that summons you out of your temporary despair into a renewed desire to go on living. It is that which keeps you going through the night until the time when you can see and think more clearly.

Loneliness is very different from being alone. You can be in a crowd and still experience loneliness. Loneliness is a longing to be reunited with what you once knew—the love that you once experienced, the companionship you once had that gave you a sense of security. Loneliness happens to young people when they venture from home for the first time and they are faced with new situations with which they must deal. Loneliness happens when you travel afar off to places with which you are not familiar. It happens when you celebrate holidays outside of the normal traditions to which you have become accustomed. It even happens when you suddenly find yourself assuming responsibilities that were not previously yours.

What then is the root of loneliness? Loneliness is a passive state into which you sometimes allow yourself to fall. It is a feeling of emptiness and longing. If you do nothing but fret and you allow yourself to remain passive, you will remain lonely and possibly become severely depressed and despondent.

But, fortunately, there are cures for loneliness. That is why you must consider that which is lovely. God has provided you with the ability to take action. He has created within you a drive for action. As you listen to that voice within, and as you move yourself into action of some sort, your lonely state begins to dissipate.

A primary aspect of dissipating loneliness is to recognize it and express it. Your expressions can be via a telephone call to another person, through writing a poem, singing a song, praying, or even talking aloud to yourself. As you express your feelings of loneliness, you often find you are frustrated, angry, or sad. As you acknowledge these feelings, you can take action to change them. If the loneliness is over the loss of the one you have loved so dearly for years, you might take his or her picture and talk to them, or you might sit down and review the memories that you shared. Some may use art or poetry to release these feelings. The important thing is to stop being passive and become more active. The moment you do this is the moment your spirit begins to be renewed and you find new hope for the time ahead.

Although loneliness is painful, if you realize that God has already provided you with the means to renew your hope then you have learned a lesson of great value. You can share that lesson with others who also may experience such feelings.

> The best remedy for those who are afraid, lonely or unhappy is to go outside, somewhere where they can be quiet, alone with the heavens, nature and God. Because only then does one feel that all is as it should be and that God wishes to see people happy, amidst the simple beauty of nature. Frank, February 23, 1944

To Dream a Dream

When in the course of life,
Men have woven a dream.
Their world has changed from commonplace
To sites of great esteem.

Without a dream, all hope will fade
And life will soon grow old.
But with a dream your world will live,
And dreams will soon take hold.

For life is really made of dreams
That oftentimes come true
As dreamers carve their steps in stone
And many goals pursue.

So if within you lives a dream
But it seems far away,
Hold that dream within your heart;
It will be real someday!

Helen S. Peterson

When Loneliness Incapacitates You . . .
Consider that which is lovely!

Experiencing loneliness when you find yourself left alone is quite normal. But, you may suffer from loneliness to the point of feeling incapacitated. What do you do when this happens? Some folks try to fill the void by playing computer games, reading, sleeping, or even just wandering about in their home or car. Others just sit and do nothing at all. Of course, none of these activities addresses the major need—the emptiness inside—and these activities can be a waste of time and energy.

Many people pretend they feel just great when friends ask them, but generally they are not truthful. It is not that they can't be by themselves; it is just that they love that sense of completeness that comes when someone else cherishes them and is by their side as their companion. But, when you acknowledge your loneliness publically, there sometimes is a sense of shame that you self-inflict by such openness. You often think that some people will consider you to be weak.

Many times, people who suffer this great loneliness cry out to God in anger. They question the fairness of it all. They wonder why their friends have not been treated in the same way. Sometimes they even think God has been cruel, especially because not knowing how to handle new situations and tasks in life makes them feel vulnerable.

Is there really anything that is lovely about struggling with loneliness and empty feelings?

Yes! Definitely. During these times you may find that you cry out to God in a real way. You may find yourself being more honest with Him than you have ever been. At these times that you may stretch your faith to believe that God has a plan. You may *know* His promises, but you may have forgotten them. He said, "For I know the plans I have for you . . . plans to prosper you and to give you hope and a future" Jeremiah 29:11(NIV).

It is terribly hard, but absolutely wonderful to grow through these times of pain. Yet, later, when others speak to you of their pain, you have a slight understanding of what they are talking about. What a blessing it is to others when you can articulate the feelings that they have but are afraid to express. What a bond of friendship that creates.

While it is difficult, you can gain so much by walking in the valley for a while. Here you cannot be overly occupied with what you think is important because you do not have the energy to do so. You merely can go from one day to another, living the best way that you know how at the moment. Sometimes it seems as though you are walking in the midst of a great cloud. You cannot see much beyond the fringes of the cloud. But, even that is lovely because when the sun does shine through, when things change, life is so much more beautiful than you had remembered.

What a blessing it is to be taught by God through the hard times of life. What a blessing it is to walk beside God during those times—or perhaps it is He who walks beside us. What a blessing it is to be chosen by God to participate in some of the sorrows that Christ and the Father felt as Christ lived here on this earth separated from the Heavenly Father. What a privilege it is to be able to bear the sorrow that would have been another's if you had been the one God called from this life first.

In all things you can give thanks to God who is good and gracious. This life here on earth is but a prelude to the life that will be for eternity. You are becoming sanctified through your sorrows and by the love of God in your life. For those who suffer loneliness, this is but a part of the sanctification process.

Don't miss the blessings by trying to avoid the pain. You cannot avoid the pain because it is a part of the healing process. Instead, you can be deliberate. When you look all around you for that which is lovely, you will be sure to rid yourself of loneliness and find beauty where you least expect it.

I Wandered Lonely as a Cloud

> I wandered lonely as a cloud
> That floats on high o'er vales and hills,
> When all at once I saw a crowd,
> A host, of golden daffodils;
> Beside the lake, beneath the trees,
> Fluttering and dancing in the breeze.
>
> Continuous as the stars that shine
> And twinkle on the Milky Way,
> They stretched in never-ending line
> Along the margin of a bay:
> Ten thousand saw I at a glance,
> Tossing their heads in sprightly dance.
>
> The waves beside them danced; but they
> Outdid the sparkling waves in glee:

A poet could not but be gay,
In such a jocund company:
I gazed—and gazed—but little thought
What wealth the show to me had brought:

For oft, when on my couch I lie
In vacant or in pensive mood,
They flash upon that inward eye
Which is the bliss of solitude;
And then my heart with pleasure fills,
And dances with the daffodils.
Wordsworth

When All You Want Is That Old Relationship . . .
Consider that which is lovely!

Marriage, no matter how happy or how difficult it may have been, was a relationship to which you gave, and from which you received, something. Sometimes, in your grief, you feel guilt or sorrow that the relationship was not all that you had desired or perhaps expected. Maybe you feel some guilt that you did not do all you think you could have to make the time richer. Regardless of your regrets, the loss of that relationship still leaves you empty and alone.

As you ponder the years of marriage or friendship, perhaps you wonder where the time was spent, and why you put so much emphasis on "succeeding." You may admonish yourself for having been somewhat selfish about getting your way. You may chastise yourself, unjustly, for having taken time for yourself or for your friends instead of spending it with your loved one. Perhaps you may wish that you had expressed your love and appreciation more frequently.

One of the grand and truly wonderful aspects of loss is that through it, you realize that loving relationships, filled with integrity and trust, are what make us wealthy. Above all, it is lovely if you will realize that your relationship with God is paramount to having any successful or really fulfilling loving relationships with your spouse or anyone else.

As you go through your time of grieving, when you desire relationships that are rich and satisfying, perhaps one of the greatest gifts that you can receive from the pain of your grief is a new understanding that the focus of your life needs to be on the simple life, filled with sincere appreciation for those who are already a part of your life, and for those new persons who come in to help fill the void of your loss.

> Lord,
> We ask that through our grief you open our eyes
> to see the beauty in those around us.
> Free us from guilt or regret which simply rob us of our energy.
> Help us to grow more mature in all of our relationships.
> Let us love honestly and deeply as you also love us. Amen

Simplify

Our journey through life begins simply
But often becomes a chore
As we add to our list the things we want
And abandon the things before.

We find ourselves fast moving
To keep up with the rest,
And give up loving treasures
Believing more is best.

We frantically travel through the years
Seeking goods and fame,
And only glance, but briefly,
To view the futile game.

But when at last, we come to rest
Our weary race all done,
We then begin to understand
That game could not be won.

Often late do we realize,
As we glimpse the far-off shore,
Our journey through life is richest
As we love each other more!

Helen S. Peterson

When Pining Overcomes You . . .
Consider that which is lovely!

Various dictionary definitions define pining as having a powerful desire for something. Pining is not only deep passion or a desire, but it also includes the notion of physical or emotional suffering as a result of the real or apparent hopelessness of one's desire.

Many times when you lose someone you loved, you pine to have them back with you or just to hear their voice or see their face "one more time." Such emotional behavior is common to those who have been with the loved one consistently as in the case of spouses.

Pining takes a great deal of energy from you. It is not that you are doing things that are so physically difficult, but when you are using up the chemicals in your body that help you to produce emotion, you are using the physical resources that your body has available. Many of those same chemicals provide energy for you to do other things. Very often, when you pine for that which is impossible, you are not otherwise occupied with some productive chore. Rather, you may be sitting lifelessly in a chair or still lying in your bed. Often you go around as though you are in a cloud, not being able to think clearly or logically. That is because the right side of your brain, which controls your emotional aspects, is interfering with the left side of your brain, which controls your logic. Hence, you can't concentrate or use your logic efficiently.

You may say that if you don't pine for your loved one, you may forget the person he or she was. Do you really think that is possible? You may feel as though you are being disloyal to that person by not keeping him or her constantly in your thoughts. Did you keep them in your thoughts *all* the time before they died? I think not. You were living life and doing things that you needed or wished to do.

By pining, you are endangering your own physical and emotional health. Your body is under constant stress, perhaps more stress than it may be able to bear. Eventually you may find yourself in a full-blown state of depression. Do you really wish for this to happen just because you may be making poor choices about how to deal with your grief?

How can you change the pining into something that is positive? After all, God wants you to consider that which is lovely. The lovely part of this behavior is that you can take control of it. You can make the choice to resist the urge to pine your life away over something that can never be again. You can make yourself accept that death is final. It is finished. It is finished because that one you loved has now completed his or her mission on this earth. Regardless of how the death came, whether it was after a prolonged illness, after a sudden heart attack or stroke, or perhaps after a traumatic accident, the fact is your loved one's life on earth is now complete. He or she has successfully done whatever it was that God planned for them to do when He placed them on this earth. When you are willing to accept that fact, then you will be able to overcome your need to pine after him or her. When you realize that you are in control over your own emotional state, you have come a long way toward healing from grief. What is more important is that this understanding of the control you have will enable you to take control in other areas of your life. And that, my friend, is a lovely thing to know and to feel.

As you take control, you will find that your desire to rejoin life will reignite. You will begin to take an interest in things you used to like, and perhaps, even in some new things. In the long run, you will feel as though you have accomplished a great deal and that you have grown into a new, and probably, a better person.

A Letter from Your Loved One:

My Beloved,

You were an inspiration and a joy to me while I lived there on earth. I am sure that you miss me now that I have a new life. You will be here one day. Please be aware it is important to all of us here to know you will fulfill your mission on earth. Sometimes we can see what you are not able to see with mortal eyes. We can see the tapestry of your life as you go on living. In some places it appears dark, but in so many places it is aglow with rich color. How we wish you knew the treasures that are ahead for you. Go on with life, my Beloved. I will be here waiting with open arms when you are called to complete your mortal days and enter the heavenly eternity.

Signed,
Your Devoted Love

Moving beyond Yearning . . .

                                                Consider that which is lovely!

Perhaps you have experienced a hollow pain deep inside for your deceased loved one even when you are with people you know and love. There you were, in the middle of a group, quietly masking the inner ache, listening as others around you engaged in jovial conversation, sometimes even making your own comments to add to the joviality. How difficult it is when you have lost a person whom you have loved, but the whole world around you seems to forget while you continue to ache inside.

Some of your ache may actually be a *yearning*. Yearning is a kind of wishful thinking for things that really can or might never be. Yearning takes so much energy, but yet produces no positive results. Basically, it is a state of mind that tends to inhibit forward movement.

What can you do to think differently about your situation? How can you turn your feelings of loneliness or yearning into that which is lovely? The key is in whether you really wish to do so. It is not an easy task to change your feelings or your perceptions of your situation.

However, let us consider these things: When you are lonely, you may choose to brood and to accomplish nothing, or you may choose to look inside of yourself to discover new talents, abilities, and gifts that you have not used before. Try to think of things you may always have wanted to do or to be and decide if this may be the time to try some of those things. It may not be easy at first, but God wants you to know yourself better. If you ask, He will guide your thoughts to help you discover hidden talents and abilities. By developing these, you will acquire a new sense of yourself. Your new awareness will spur you on into new activities and perhaps, even new friends. Local colleges or continuing education programs may be places you can investigate to nurture some new interests.

When you realize that yearning will not bring back what used to be, then you have reached a stage of *acceptance*. Facing the truth and accepting the finality brings a great deal of peace because you now realize that your life *must* go on, not as it was before, but in a new manner. The internal turmoil, the wrestling with your thoughts and emotions, generally stops when you are able to face reality. It is then that you find the "good side" of loneliness and yearning. Your newfound sense of freedom is then the signal for you to make some new plans for a "new normal" life.

If you have not been a particularly outgoing person before the death of your loved one, you may choose to become more so. Should you choose to involve yourself with new, more solitary projects, that, too, will be outstanding.

Loneliness and yearning can be the keys to a new life. The only part of life over which you really have control is your ability to make choices. If you wish to go on living life fully, you must choose to make it happen.

Walking through Grief and Sorrow

Walking through the midst of grief and sorrow
I paused, for a gentle voice spoke my name.
In hushed penetration came the message
Of hope and cheer.
"Fear not, for I alone bring release from pain."

Somewhere in the echoes of my memory,
It seemed I had traveled this path before . . .
Ah, yes! Not once, but several times.
Sometimes alone, sometimes with
Another sorrowing soul.

And now, was I alone?
Or did there seem to be a hand in mine?
I waited in quiet expectancy, sensing that soon
My soul would spring to life again—
That soon I would be able to see with new vision!

And then it came. That soothing balm, that loving
Gentle peace, enveloping my being,
Wrapping His strong arms about me.
Praise to the Almighty!
He stooped to lift *me* to a higher plane
And bring to life new joy!

Helen S. Peterson

Looking for a New Relationship . . .
Consider that which is lovely!

Because the process of grieving is painful and seemingly unending, many people prefer to end that pain by looking for a new partner to fill the emptiness. Generally, this desire is because you have not lived alone for a long while, and learning to live with yourself is a difficult task. There are new chores and new decisions that you are required to make alone. There are household tasks and maintenance with which you have not been acquainted. There are social experiences that you have not encountered by yourself before. Overall, you long for the time when your loved one was there to do these things with you so that the sense of responsibility or the sense of aloneness might not weigh so heavily upon you.

There is also the problem of not having someone with whom to talk, or in whom to confide some of your most precious thoughts. There is the problem of learning to go to bed alone at night. There is the problem of learning to cook meals for just one person, if you even feel like eating. The list goes on and on, and you simply do not like to live life by yourself. It is too painful. It is too hard and too empty.

A mistake that you may make at this vulnerable time in your life is to seek out someone who seems to be similar to your deceased loved one, either in physical characteristics or in personality makeup. However, in seeking a substitute for your deceased loved one, sometimes you rationalize and often assign characteristics to the new person that really don't exist, except in your own mind. You welcome conversation and often go beyond conversation into physical relationships. Your mind becomes confused by your emotions, which, to begin with, are not functioning in a balanced manner. You start to believe that you are hopelessly in love, no matter if you are forty years old or ninety years old. Often, you then enter into a serious relationship and maybe even marriage before knowing yourself or the other person well enough. You do what you would not have allowed your teenagers to do, under the belief that now you are mature and you do not need to take time to make a more thorough examination of what you have chosen.

In some instances, these relationships may be smooth and work well. In others, after a few weeks or months, there are severe disappointments because of your preconceived expectations.

How can you think lovely things about this period in your life when you are so uncomfortable with the new lifestyle into which you have been forced? It is wonderful to realize that changes require you to grow. Growth is painful, but it yields bountiful rewards. When you learn how to care for yourself in ways that you did not know how to do before, you gain a sense of control over your life. This sense of control is so valuable at a time when life events have been very much out of your control. When you push yourself to enter into social situations alone, often you find that you are much more able to function than you had thought you were. This adds to your sense of well-being. When you take the time to know yourself, in spite of your loneliness, you often emerge as a more healthy human being, with more character, more integrity, more maturity, and overall, more to offer another person when you finally do begin another serious relationship. Waiting through the time of painful adaptation to your new life may be difficult, but from that waiting period you can emerge, just as a lovely flower emerges in the springtime from the ground, with new beauty and purpose, unlike that which you had before.

> "For everything there is an appointed time, and an appropriate time for every activity on earth: a time to be born, and a time to die; a time to plant, and a time to uproot what was planted; a time to kill, and a time to heal; a time to break down, and a time to build up; a time to weep, and a time to laugh; a time to mourn, and a time to dance."
> -Ecclesiastes 3:1–4 (New English Translation)

Needing to Feel Loved . . .
                                    Consider that which is lovely!

    In the course of your grief journey, even as you become more accustomed to being alone, you sometimes feel the need for the love of a special person in your life. Your spouse is gone, and you no longer have that companionship or affirmation of being loved and being an important part of another person's life. Oh, sometimes you have children or a relative or a friend who cares about you; but that is not the same. When you have known the intimate, caring love of a spouse, you miss it terribly. Even if that spouse was unable to show love in the manner you thought you needed it, you still miss the thought of that love. It is then that you want to seek out someone special. While you often feel the need, you also sometimes feel the guilt of "betraying" that one that whom you loved so much. You may feel as though it would be dishonoring to that spouse's memory to find someone else to love. Often you fear that you might forget that loved one. Sometimes you fear that you may never find someone as good as the spouse that you had. Sometimes you are afraid that you will make a mistake and find someone who will not treat you kindly. Sometimes you fear the disapproval of your children or others who are dear to you.

    As your thoughts and feelings begin to move in that direction, you must consider what they may mean. If you have allowed time to do the work of grief, then quite possibly you are coming to accept that your loved one is truly gone and will not return. On the other hand, if you can't deal with the pain that grief brings, you may simply want a substitute who can fill your life and take your mind from the pain that is so necessary to healthy grief. That is the reason that grief and bereavement counselors suggest that you make no major changes in your life for at least one or possibly two years after your loss. Of course, there are exceptions to that, particularly if you are older and feel as though your time in life is limited. Remember, however, that God will grant you all the time you need in this life to have joy and peace!

    How then, can you consider that this emerging need is lovely? It is, indeed, lovely to know that you have the desire to love and to be loved again. It is a time when you can realize that you are beginning to feel the need for that emotion that was so much a part of your life with your beloved spouse. It is a sign to yourself that you must carefully evaluate what you have done to face the grief and the pain. If you do such an evaluation and find that you have really learned to live alone, that you have, indeed, changed into a more mature person as a result of your loss, and that you have endured the pain of growth through grief, then you can feel proud of yourself that you are now a new person, ready to go on into another phase of life.

If you do such an evaluation and find that you are running away from pain, you can then counsel yourself to wait and grow. Unfortunately, most of us who run from pain, do not want to take the time required to really heal. But, if for a short while, you can switch into your intellectual mode of behavior, you can often avert a poor decision based on need. You can seek out wise counsel to help you to slow down your decision-making process and to face what you need to face so that in the future you are more mature both emotionally and spiritually.

It is God's will that you keep all things in balance. That includes the need to be loved. He has promised that when you are feeling that need, He himself will meet that need in His own way. Remember, Jesus Christ lived on this earth. He was a man with emotional needs as much as He was God. He must have struggled with those needs to be loved or He would not understand your needs today. You can trust Him when He refers to you as "His chosen bride." He can and will provide for your needs, for He knows what they are, and He loves His children dearly.

"I will not leave you comfortless. I will come to you."
-John 14:18 (KJV)

After the Heavy Load Is Carried

Though at times the load is heavy,
And it seems too hard to bear;
Though we often feel so hopeless
Wondering if there is a God who cares,
Though our anger and our sadness
Seem to overwhelm our soul,
Though we feel that life is empty
And we never can be whole,
Though there is a time of weeping,
And a time to live through grief,
Again there will be joyfulness,
And times of blessed relief.
Again we will find meaning

Loneliness

In life's never ending quest.
Again we will be filled with love
And find we've passed the test.
Again we will hear the laughter
And the joyful sounds of life;
Again we will be able
To live above the strife.

       Helen S. Peterson

When You Think That God Has Deserted You . . .
Consider that which is lovely!

The story is told of the only survivor of a shipwreck who was washed up on a small, uninhabited island. He prayed feverishly for God to rescue him, and every day he scanned the horizon for help, but none seemed forthcoming. Exhausted, he eventually managed to build a little hut out of driftwood to protect him from the elements and to store his few possessions.

But then one day, after scavenging for food, he arrived home to find his little hut in flames, the smoke rolling up to the sky. The worst had happened—everything was lost. He was stunned with grief and anger.

"God, how could you do this to me?" he cried. Early the next day, however, he was awakened by the sound of a ship that was approaching the island. Much to his surprise and great delight, it had come to rescue him.

"How did you know I was here?" asked the weary man of his rescuers.

"We saw your smoke signal," they replied.

God sees all the smoke signals that you are sending up as you go through these days of grieving and mourning. His rescue ship is on the way. But, in His infinite wisdom, He has designed you so that your healing comes slowly but surely, if you are willing to travel the path of suffering. The pathway of suffering is not all sadness and tears. Some days you have joy and laughter. Some days you feel as though you can conquer the world. Some days you know that life will be okay again. But there are the days of emptiness and discouragement when you just want to be by yourself and not speak a word to any other human being. There are days when you leave the shelter of your secure place, only to return and find yourself in greater distress.

The lovely thing about this period of waiting is that it is also a period of growth. You find your mind and body taxed to the limits to achieve small, somewhat inconsequential tasks of life, and yet somehow you make it through your days and nights. You often hate to yield yourself to a state of dependence, but when you do, you find that so many people love you and are willing to give you support and love. You find that it is not so awful to become a little dependent because in becoming so, you become an example of strength and courage to others who follow you. You learn that without your loved one life is very hard, but that memories of times together can be a strong source of joy and encouragement. You learn that you can conquer things that you never believed you were able to do. And most important, this period of waiting and growing helps you to depend upon your God to sustain you through the pangs of sorrow and growth.

The healing of mind, body, and spirit generally takes time. God designed it that way for a purpose. He could have made you differently. He could have provided instant healing for all wounds. Our understanding is too limited to know the reason He chose the way He did. Yet, as you accept the way it is, and wait patiently with faith and hope for better days, you will certainly reap the reward of greater wisdom, more patience, greater sensitivity to the losses of others, and deeper understanding of the complexities of God and His loving ways.

> "Three times I pleaded with the Lord to take it (*Paul's infirmity*) away from me. But he said to me, 'My grace is sufficient for you, for my power is made perfect weakness.' Therefore I will boast all the more gladly about my weaknesses, so that Christ's power may rest on me."
> -2 Corinthians 12:8–9 (NIV)

Another Way to Go

> Would that I could
> Change things that in my world
> Have gone awry.
> But who am I,
> That I should think I could change
> All that is amiss?
> Yet all is not undone. I am one
> Who can change myself to accept
> That which I cannot control
> And to change that which I can.
> Life goes on.
> Change precedes needed growth.
> That which has gone awry is now history.
> And I, yes, I can make new history.
>
> Helen S. Peterson

When Your Days Weigh Heavily and Your Nights Are Worse . . .
Consider that which is lovely!

Sometimes, when you lose your loved one, it is difficult to find comfort any time of day or night. You may not sleep well during the night and then want to sleep all day long. You may not be able to sleep either day or night. You may find ways to make the days pass, but when the darkness comes, you may become anxious for no apparent reason. You may be afraid to go to sleep because when you do, you have nightmares. Instead you may stay up watching television or working on your computer. You may try to read until you are so tired you can't stay awake. When there is no one else in the house with you, nighttime is very lonely. You hesitate to call anyone to tell them of your fear and loneliness because you do not want to disturb them. You also feel that you are being foolish feeling this way.

Be assured that what you are experiencing is a very normal part of grieving. Although it is not pleasant, it will pass. As you become more accepting of the finality of your loss, and as you become more accustomed to being by yourself, you will begin to relax and not experience the fear or anxiety that keeps you awake.

It is wonderful to know that there are things you can do to help yourself. You can be very consistent about going to bed at the same time every night and getting up at the same time every day. Such behavior begins to set a new pattern for you. Even when you are extremely tired during the day, you must stay awake until it is bedtime. You can do something pleasant before you go to bed. Read your Bible or read a good book. Put on calming music to help you fall asleep. Be sure that where you sleep is pleasant and that there is fresh air in the room. Make some plans for the next day so that when you go to sleep you have something to look forward to.

You might be tempted to rely on prescription medication. If it is possible not to do that, then that is better. Very often medications prevent you from dreaming or else they trigger nightmares. Dreams are an essential means by which your brain reorganizes your experiences and help you to deal with reality. Warm milk before bedtime sometimes helps to settle you. Of course, if medication is needed, you should take some, but always do so under a medical doctor's care.

Eventually you will sleep again. Eventually life will resume and you will feel "normal" again. Be patient. Healing from loss does not come overnight. But joy comes in the morning.

"Weeping may remain for a night, but rejoicing comes in the morning."
Psalm 30:5 (NIV)

Father in Heaven,

My night has been filled with misery. All I could do was toss and turn. I am in agony, and I do not know how to find your peace. Fill me now with your comfort. I need to know you care. I open myself to your Spirit. I believe. I know that this suffering is nothing compared to that which your Son suffered here on earth. He understands what I feel. Let him make petition on my behalf. Thank you, Father, for Your healing balm. Amen.

Courage for Life

Without an understanding of life's hardest times,
We would go undaunted and live with hapless minds.
But with the times behind us, and many still ahead,
We know we can have courage, with nothing great to dread.

The times of pain and sorrow, the times that are so hard,
They make the way for faith and hope and gaining trust in God.
They broaden our compassion and deepen hope we feel.
If again we journey through this way, we know that we will heal.

Yet times of pain and sorrow, of disappointment, loss and woe
Are awfully hard to understand, and often tears will flow.
The darkness seems so threatening; the questions never end.
The pain seems so unbearable that even sleep is not a friend.

Quite often in these times of pain we feel so all alone
As if the world's abandoned us, and we must bear it on our own.
In these times of desperation we can only turn to God.
He understands the pain we feel, for on this earth He trod.

When finally we stop trying to make some sense of pain,
We often find the answers come; the suffering's not in vain.
It is when we look behind us, and see the pattern clear,
That we can smile once again, and put away our fear.

Helen S. Peterson

When You Make Poor Choices because of Loneliness . . .
Consider that which is lovely!

Sometimes, in your loneliness, you search for ways to make you feel better. At times you begin eating too much or drinking too much. Perhaps you seek relationships that really are harmful rather than helpful. Sometimes you make large purchases such as a new car or truck, a new tractor, or new clothing that are not really needed at the time. Yes, even Christians look to alcohol, drugs, sexual behavior, or spending too much money to fill the emptiness that exists because of the loss that has occurred. In your time of grief and bereavement, you may rationalize that it is okay for you to indulge yourself since you need some relief from the pain of loneliness.

However, it is *not* okay, and you know it is not okay to do those things that are self-destructive. Each time you make a decision to involve yourself in actions that you really do not believe are good and healthy, or ones that you feel are not in God's will, you prolong the resolution of your grief and add more to the load that you are carrying already. It is in these times that you need to depend upon the clarity of God's truth within so that when issues in life are so chaotic and distorted, you can make healthy and wholesome choices. Sometimes those choices mean that you will live, for a brief time, with pain and loneliness until you adapt to your life without your loved one.

You are not alone through this time of confusion and loneliness. It is lovely to know that God has told us that He "will never leave us nor forsake us" Hebrews. 13:9 (KJV). By consciously making those choices that are spiritually, physically, and emotionally healthy, you begin to understand the strength that you have from within. As you overcome making unhealthy choices, you then understand what it means when the Apostle Paul tells us "I can do all things through Christ who strengthens me" (Phil. 4:13). Just by being willing to endure a temporary time of suffering in this life, you will find that it is wonderful to become more mature and more in tune with your precious Lord.

> "His divine power has given us everything we need for life and godliness through our knowledge of him."
>
> -2 Peter 1:3 (NIV)

"The Lord delights in the way of a man whose steps he has made firm; though he stumble, he will not fall, for the Lord upholds him with his hand."

-Psalm 37:23-24 (NIV)

Father,

I am lonely. I hurt deeply. I want the pain to go away, and because of it I am tempted to do things that I know are not good for me just in order to get relief from the pain. However, I have faith that you are with me right now. You understand my needs. Please keep me safe from myself. Hold me closely. Place your loving arms around me and comfort me. Make me willing to be willing to wait for your time of healing. Teach me what action I need to take to obtain the healing you want to supply. Thank you, God. Amen.

When Loneliness Can Be a Blessing . . .
Consider that which is lovely!

When you have lost someone whom you loved dearly, you will no doubt experience loneliness. Loneliness is not a feeling that you can chase away by activity, by being surrounded by loving people, or by keeping yourself so busy that you can't think about the loss. Loneliness is a feeling that is present with you even in a crowded place such as Times Square, New York, surrounded by thousands of people, some of whom are your friends or relatives. It goes to sleep with you, and it awakens with you. It is the realization that a part of you is now missing and has not been healed. It is the sad feeling inside that you will never meet another person in this world who was exactly like the one whom you lost. You will never see all those qualities that you loved, packaged together in one person again. It is the result of the risk you took when you chose to love that person. In order not to experience loneliness, you may choose to place a protective shell around you that does not allow a single individual or pet to enter. Since most of us do not choose to do this, almost all of us will experience loneliness at some time in our lives.

Does God understand loneliness? I venture to say that He does. When God sent a part of Himself to this earth for thirty-three years, I believe that it must have given Him great pain to be separated and to see His Son living here on this Planet Earth that was tainted by sin. When He watched His son dying on a cross it must have given Him great sadness to know that He would have to turn His back on Him. And when the Father did turn His back, the Son also experienced great loneliness. He knew He had to do the job alone, as hard it may have been.

How can you turn the experience of loneliness into something that is lovely? You must choose to do that. You can turn to the Holy Father, who has told us we have His Holy Spirit on this earth with us to be our Comforter. You can ask for that comfort, and because God loves you, He will provide comfort for your loneliness. You can choose to thank God for the fact that you had that loved one on this earth to create memories and to share love however short or long that may have been. Out of a grateful heart comes praise. When you praise God for all that you do have, you receive relief from the feelings you are experiencing. You can empathize with others who may also be alone and lonely. When you give yourself to others, healing begins. You can be grateful for the experience of loneliness so that you are able to empathize with credibility. And, when you are able, you can turn your feelings of loneliness into projects of love to help others in this world survive the pitfalls and the pain.

Sabrina Beasley McDonald is the author of *Open the Windows of Heaven*, a women's devotional, and *The Blessings of Loneliness*. Sabrina is a former senior writer and web editor for Family Life, a marriage and family ministry of Cru (Campus Crusade for Christ), working mainly with Family Life's online magazine *The Family Room*.

She became a stay-at-home mom and freelance writer in 2008 when her first child was born. In 2010, her first husband was killed in a car accident, leaving her as a single mom of two young children. In July 2013, she married Robbie McDonald, also widowed, and gained two stepsons and a daughter-in-law, as well.

As a college student she experienced extreme loneliness as she watched her friends marrying and having children. At long last, God blessed her with a wonderful husband, David, and after a short while God took him from her. After David's sudden accidental death, she lived for three years in a shroud of loneliness trying her best to raise her two small children. In her book, *The Blessings of Loneliness* (Chisel Books, September 16, 2004), Sabrina McDonald encourages women who are single, prior to a marriage or as widows, to go through the pain of loneliness rather than run from it by involving oneself in all sorts of activities that tend to distract. She suggests throughout her writing it is not the loneliness that becomes the blessing, but rather the positive fruits of that loneliness that make one's life rich. She reiterates how she came to know God in a deeper and more intimate relationship as a result of her loneliness, and she encourages all women who are lonely to seek Him.

Having been in a similar situation, I can testify to the fact that God does meet our emotional, spiritual and physical needs when we turn to him in our loneliness. That new relationship with God is a beautiful one; one sometimes missed when we are still married or in a loving relationship with another. When we have humans on whom we can depend, we sometimes neglect that same relationship with God and miss the joyful intimacy only He can provide.

It may sound "flowery" to suggest that God can actually take the place of a loved one, but, it is important to remember your widowhood is no surprise to God. He was well aware of the fact that you would lose the one you loved. He intends for us to know Him in a more personal manner. Sometimes the only way we achieve that dependency is through adversity and loss. He has said, "I will never leave you nor forsake you so we can confidently say, 'The Lord is my helper; I will not fear; what can man do to me?'" Hebrews 13:6(ESV)

"The Lord says: 'Do not cling to events of the past or dwell on what happened long ago. Watch for the new thing I am going to do. It is happening already—you can see it now. I will make a road through the wilderness and give you streams of water there.'"
-Isaiah 43:18–19 (Good News Translation)

God On the Mountain

Life is easy, when you're up on the mountain
And you've got peace of mind, like you've never known.
But things change, when you're down in the valley.
Don't lose faith, for you're never alone.

For the God on the mountain, is the God in the valley.
When things go wrong, He'll make them right.
And the God of the good times
Is still God in the bad times.
The God of the day is still God in the night.

We talk of faith way up on the mountain.
Talk comes so easy when life's at its best.
Now down in the valleys, of trials and temptations
That's where your faith, is really put to the test.

For the God on the mountain is the God in the valley.
When things go wrong, He'll make them right.
And the God of the good times
is still God in the bad times.
The God of the day, is still God in the night.
The God of the day, is still God in the night.

(Lynda Randle, God on the Mountain, by Tracy Dartt, Spring House Productions Inc. c.2005, manufactured by Gaither Music Group, Alexandria, IN, compact disc.)

Pain

You Detest the Pain and Suffering of Grief . . .
Consider that which is lovely!

In this life, pain and suffering never go away. Sometimes they ease, and there are periods when you feel better than others, but overall, pain and suffering are an integral part of the human experience. There is some pain from which you are able to heal entirely. But other pain, such as that incurred by the loss of loved ones can leave a wound from which you may never heal completely. That being the case, achieving the most healing as a result of our grieving process is of extremely great value.

The pain you suffer now can either make you *bitter* or *better.* When you become *bitter*, your attitude cannot remain hidden from those who love you deeply and who are able "to look right inside of you." A good façade may fool the world, but the ones who love you deeply often see you better than you see yourself. When you are *better*, the whole world is able to see your gentle spirit, your calmness in the midst of the storms, your joy of living in spite of the pain, your eager desire to grow and to keep on living life to the fullest degree, your empathy for those who also are suffering, and your desire to encourage them through life's storms.

The loveliness that comes from this pain is that you can choose to become much better, rather than mean and bitter. In order to do so, you must acknowledge your pain—to yourself, to understanding friends, and to God. You must learn to accept the grace that God bestows upon you through the love of your friends and those around you. You must accept that pain is a normal part of this life and gladly take up your "cross" and walk the pathway of suffering. Remember, Christ never said "Jump into your Mercedes and follow me." He told us, instead, to "take up your cross and follow me" Matthew 16:24(ESV)). Healing comes not from *running away* from pain and suffering, regardless if it is physical or emotional. Healing comes not from *pretending* you do not hurt. Healing comes not from completely *eliminating* the pain. Rather, healing comes directly from acknowledging your pain, living through it while you are healing, and growing from the experience.

Christ's example to us was that of an individual who endured incredible suffering and pain, not just through death, but also through life. He grieved over rejection from his own family, the pain of isolation, the pain of homelessness and dependence, the pain of the death of his own earthly Dad, the pain of leaving his mom without the son whose duty it was to take care of his mother, the pain of watching his friends make mistakes, and the pain of watching those to whom he offered healing, turn away from it.

Pain

You may ask: "How did he gain that which was lovely from the pain of His grief?" He accepted the nature of His human existence. He was realistic about the fact that pain exists as a part of that experience. In doing so, He was not a victim of it, but instead grew and matured through it. Instead of allowing Himself to be the victim of pain, He became the victor over it. Even though He was the Son of God, humanly He still had to learn patience, wisdom, endurance and maturity. He knew he still had to learn to deal with disappointments and the shortcomings of life without becoming bitter about all of them.

You do not have to *like* pain and suffering to grow from it. You just have to *not hate* it in order to grow from it. You have to live patiently as you pass through it. You must acknowledge honestly, that even in the midst of pain, there are moments of great joy and great insight. You have to believe that once the greatest pain has passed, life again will have some peaceful times. You must recognize that you do not suffer alone in your grief and that few in the world escape it. You must be willing to accept the pain-filled times and to realize that there is meaning in whatever you happen to be doing at the moment.

You know that healing is happening when you begin to prioritize your values as a result of the suffering and pain. You know that healing is happening when you are able to express your love toward others openly. It is happening when you learn how to be interdependent: both independent and dependent. Healing is happening when you are able to share your burdens with others, knowing there is more strength in weakness than there is in strength alone. When you use your faith to produce hope for the future and whatever it holds, you are proving that you are healing, to yourself and to others. You know that healing is happening when you realize again that there is purpose and meaning to everything you do no matter how menial or unimportant that task seems to be. Even when you know there is no complete cure for the pain, then bitterness will not set in. You can learn, with Paul, to be content in whatever state or condition you find yourself, and you can take delight in the opportunity to grow more like our example, Jesus Christ.

Feeling Sad

> When your heart is filled with sadness
> And your soul is wrapped in grief,
> There seems no sweet illusion
> To bring your soul relief.

Your voice is sadly moaning;
Your heart feels broken, too.
You don't have any answers
To tell you what to do.

You try with all that's in you
To heal the hurting wound,
But it is to no avail
With reminders all around.

And so you go on hurting;
So few who know your pain.
You live each moment as it comes
With the sunshine, and the rain.

You feel that you are all alone,
That no one cares about your plight.
The battle now seems endless
As you struggle through the night.

It's time for you to rest in God.
Let Him comfort you anew
For He has promised that He cares
And that He cares for *you*.

Helen S. Peterson

When the Pain Seems Too Hard to Bear . . .
Consider that which is lovely!

Pain is inevitable in life. When you lose a loved one, you feel emotional pain because of the many losses associated with the departure of that one. Your loss involves not only the companionship of the person you have loved, but also secondary losses such as status, relationships with others, potential income, and a sense of identity. When you have spent many hours together with that loved one, the pain of loneliness may become a very pertinent factor. You no longer have someone to talk with, to laugh with or to accompany you to various events and occasions. You may find yourself living alone and spending many hours in the house by yourself.

Yes, when you take the risk to love someone, you also take the risk to endure pain. But, while pain is inevitable, suffering is optional. In his book, *Enjoy Life: Healing with Happiness*, Dr. Lynn D. Johnson makes an important point that when your thoughts change (regarding situations in life) your world also changes around you. He advocates thinking positively about those situations in life that might cause you to sink into depression and despair.

How, then, can you take the pain of grief and turn it into something lovely? By thinking positively, you develop a sense of optimism. Dr. Lynn Johnson says that optimistic people think this way: "Good things last a long time, bad passes away quickly. Good events are caused by me, bad just happens. Good stuff spreads, bad experiences are limited" Lynn D. Johnson, PhD., 11.

If good things really do last a long time, then it is lovely to know that your good memories will remain with you. Focus on those. While not all that is good is the result of what you may or may not do, if many good events are brought about by your choices, then at least in part it is lovely to know that you still are able to choose to do those things that have always been satisfying. Remember that you did nothing to bring about the death of your loved one. In fact, you probably did much to help prevent it sooner. If good "stuff spreads," then it is lovely to be able to expect that your positive attitude will carry you through the pain.

Suffering is typically agony, misery, or woe. You do not have to suffer if you recognize that pain is only temporary or that you can do things within your control to alleviate some of that pain. However, you must live through some aspects of the pain of grief. That is how God created you. But, it is lovely to realize that grief does not last forever. It typically has an end if you allow yourself to heal. Life can take on new meaning and new excitement. However, if you insist on remaining in agony because you feel helpless, guilty, angry, or lonely, then your healing will take a much longer time. I remember a lady whose diabetic son died at an early age. For the next thirty years she would not allow herself to heal. Instead she lived in agony, grieving over that loss. Perhaps she also blamed herself for his death. She would not dispose of his belongings and left his bedroom in exactly the condition it was in when he died. It was only when she put away the old things and looked at his death differently that she began to heal. It is lovely to realize that you do not have to feel negative feelings. Those are choices that you make in your thinking, and you can change those choices to help yourself move along in the healing process. As you take control of your feelings, you develop a new sense of confidence and hope for the future. You realize that the pain of grief is only temporary and that the hope for a meaningful future is long lasting. It is within your control if you choose to think that way.

A Butterfly Life

> Flittering and fluttering butterflies come and go,
> Searching for the nectar in flowers by the row;
> Pollinating others as they move along the way,
> They fulfill a noble purpose as they live from day to day.
> When so very shortly their demise at last has come,
> They also meet a purpose in providing food for some.
> As humans watch them flitter, we often have great fun
> When we view their myriad colors shining in the sun.
> We can learn a lesson as we watch the butterflies;
> We can analyze *our* patterns and see us with God's eyes.
> We can be the source of food that longing souls all need.
> We can shine with lovely beauty so those around will heed.

Helen S. Peterson

Trying to Avoid the Pain of Grief . . .

Consider that which is lovely!

 Even though suffering and death were not God's original plan, He did provide you with the inner resources to deal with the pain. You tend not to use these resources as well as you might because you want to avoid pain. If you were to take all of the pain out of life, you would also have to take all the loving out of life. When you love deeply, you open yourself to become vulnerable to pain. However much you may need or want the love, you just don't want the companion, *which inevitably is pain*.

 While it is more "normal" to run from pain, I have found that the better way is to walk *with* it and *through* it. It hurts terribly, but the lessons gained from pain, suffering, and grief can be nuggets of gold. How you handle loss is what makes the difference. You can become more tender, more open, and of course, more vulnerable. You also can become a bitter, closed, and very frightened person. A third option is to try to place a shield around yourself so that you never again have to face pain. That means you do not give yourself wholeheartedly to others, you seclude yourself in your work or home, and often, you fail to experience fully new riches of loving and giving.

 Unfortunately the experience of death will never end. Death is inevitable. Our deaths and the deaths of our loved ones will continue until time is no more. God knows that. If He didn't want you and me to learn and to grow from our personal losses, then He would just take us and spare us the pain. So, my dear friend, live with your pain. Embrace it and grow with it. Do not fear pain. It will not harm you so much as running from it will. The painful times you and I experience here are so short compared to the time when you will live on the New Earth free from pain of all sorts.

 The lessons learned from patiently enduring can be so rich and precious. Rejoice that God can refine you and grow you through your experiences. Never say, "I do not ever want to go through that again," because as surely as you do say it, God will allow similar circumstances until He sees that you are completely yielded to Him. After all, there is nothing that touches your life that God has not allowed, and what He allows, He does in order for you to grow much richer, purer, emotionally stronger, and yet spiritually so much more dependent upon Him. He even allows you to make wrong decisions that bring about your own pain in order to purify you and to make you more like Him.

You might prefer to avoid pain. But, since God has so much for you to contribute to this world before you leave it, it is much wiser for you to embrace the pain that comes into your life and to grow from it. God is much too good an economist to waste the life He has given to you. He will keep you here, teaching and pruning you just as long as He needs to in order for you to fulfill the mission He has in mind for your life.

Rest in Jesus' arms and let Him carry you through the painful times of life, relying upon Him completely to provide comfort, security, love, and joy. In spite of pain, or perhaps because of the pain you are experiencing, you will learn how to live your life with excellence so that others may learn from you.

> "Heal me, O LORD, and I will be healed; Save me and I will be saved, for you are the one I praise."
>
> -Jeremiah 17:14 (NIV)

Living Life with Excellence

It's not the things that can be bought
That make our lives a treasure.
It's not the words that we might speak
Nor things that we can measure.

It's character that comes from God,
It's a spirit of faithful devotion.
It's an attitude that never gives up,
Even amidst life's great commotion.

It's living life one day at a time,
Consistently filling a place.
It's shining through darkness in this world,
Teaching others about God's grace.
It's finding the job God wants you to do,
Then working with great dedication.
It's being there one day at a time
Not seeking man's commendation.

It's faithfully, quietly living for God
A life that is pleasing to Him.
It's running the race to the very end,
And knowing the peace within.

Then when your curtain starts to fall,
And your mission you have done,
You'll have lived your life with excellence,
And His honors you'll have won.

         Helen S. Peterson

When Time Has Passed and You Still Hurt Terribly . . .
Consider that which is lovely!

Many professional counselors say that when we have passed through all the anniversaries, birthdays, and special occasions, our grief will begin to subside. Maybe that is true for some, but for many that is not the case at all. Such beliefs may only lead to disappointment. When such a time frame is set, you wonder why you are not doing better or why you are not like other people who seem to be getting on with life. When a relationship has been long and enduring, memories and thoughts of the beloved cannot be erased. Sometimes, in spite of the love, there are feelings of anger and disappointment that need to be resolved. There may be feelings of regret or guilt that an individual must face before he or she is able to let go of the pain of grief. Yes, life does go on. Although there is no way to really predict how long it will take for you to recover from the hurt, generally within two or three years you should be able to live within a new normal life. If grief continues longer, then other intervening variables may be affecting recovery from your loss.

It is not unusual to feel empty and lonely long after the special events of your life have passed. It is not unusual to long for the past although logically you know it cannot return. It is not weak or immature to feel the need to be loved and cared for, even when the relationship may not have been the most perfect one. You are created in God's image; therefore, because God loves, so do you need to love and to be loved.

How can these painful times become meaningful, lovely ones when the feeling is so intense? This emotional, and sometimes physical, pain may send us to bed in agony, or it may send us out to walk in the sunshine and fresh air. This pain may dull our senses turning our thoughts inward, or it may heighten our empathy for those who also have lost loved ones. Pain may cause us to fall into self-pity, or it may cause us to reach out to comfort those whose lives also have been wracked with pain. Pain may become the impetus for creativity or launching into new ventures. It may become the catalyst between enemies and deepened love between friends. Above all, it may bring to those who live through it new strength, new courage, and a new and better relationship with God.

If you can accept that pain is not forever, that pain is the foundation for new growth, and that pain can make us stronger, wiser, and more caring, then as you walk through your pain, you can also realize that it has a lovely side to it that you would never have known otherwise. Be strong. Have great courage. The end is in sight.

"Though I walk through the valley of the shadow of death, I will fear no evil: for thou art with me; thy rod and thy staff they comfort me."
-Psalm 23:4 (KJV)

Goodbye, Pain

Hello, dark and dismal days,
I thought that I had passed you long ago.
Pain, why don't you visit another soul?
Why must you come to me again and again?

I have tried to move ahead with life.
Pain, you have given me no relief.
When will my loss be complete?
Will I never be free from this wound?

Ah, Sunshine! You must have heard my cry.
Yes, I choose to move ahead with meaning.
I want to feel the joy of the wind at my back.
I want to walk the pathway of life again.

Pain, you may come again but you will not
Destroy my world or my vision to grow.
I am now in control of how you affect me.
I will move from dark and dismal days into the light.

Helen S. Peterson

Whammed by Grief Again . . .
Consider that which is lovely!

Just when you think you are doing great, that big wham of grief hits again. You may say to yourself, "Is this never going to end?" You may wonder why you were feeling so good and then all of a sudden you are about as low as a grasshopper's eye, seemingly unable to respond to the world around you. These feelings may come months, sometimes years, after you have lost your loved one. You then admonish yourself for getting out of control or losing it again.

Generally these feelings happen unexpectedly and with such force that they immobilize you for a brief time. In fact, the tiniest incident may trigger the greatest response. Most of the time, you may be able to face the world with a smile and you may be able to accomplish many of the things that you had been able to accomplish at other times in your life.

When you are whammed with this emotional pain you may ask, "Why is this happening?" Part of the reason for recurring pain is that you have not only lost the one you loved, but, many of your beliefs and ideas about how life should be lived, have been shattered. When your loss occurred, you moved from an *intellectual* understanding of suffering into an *experiential* understanding. Your belief system may have been telling you that loss and sorrow happen—to other people. Now you must accept that loss and sorrow happen to you. When you choose to accept that reality, your healing can take place more easily. However, there will still be some beliefs that must change, even through the years, as your experience enlightens you as to the deeper meanings of loss and suffering. From time to time, you may get "whammed" again. Take heart. These times are few and far between and last momentarily rather than over long periods.

Anna Quindlen, noted columnist and author has written these words as an explanation for why we get surprised by the pain of grief long after the event has occurred:

> Grief remains one of the few things that has the power to silence us. It is a whisper in the world and a clamor within. More than sex, more than faith, even more than its usher death, grief is unspoken, publicly ignored except for those few moments at the funeral that are over too quickly, or the conversations among the cognoscenti, those of us who recognize in one another a kindred chasm of who we are. Maybe we do not speak of it

because death will mark all of us, sooner or later, or maybe it is unspoken because grief is only the first part of it. After a time it becomes something less sharp but larger, too, a more enduring thing called loss. Perhaps that is why this is the least explored passage: because it has no end. The world loves closure, loves a thing that can, as they say, be gotten through. That is why it comes as a great surprise to find that loss is forever, that two decades after the event there are those occasions when in you cries out at the continual presence of an absence. Anna Quindlen, *The New York Times*, sect. A, p. 23 (May 4, 1994).

The lovely thing about this pain process is that when you are able to feel the pain, you are making progress toward healing, however long that may take. If you do not experience these unexpected moments of pain, then chances are that you are in strong denial or that you are trying to avoid the pain of your loss. If you allow yourself to love, then you must also realize that pain is the natural consequence of having loved. You cannot escape it. You will experience pain. It will creep out if you try to keep it under cover. And, when you try to avoid it, you stymie the victorious feeling that you can have by looking the big monster right in the eye and dealing with it. In order to get from what is in the past to what is in the future, you must go through the present. If your present is filled with denial or unreality, you will delay your growth into the future. However, by walking through the pain, you will live again.

By having unexpected moments of pain, you come to realize that a good part of your time is now spent in relatively peaceful, and maybe even enjoyable, feelings. You are far more normal than you had envisioned yourself! The interruption of your new status quo by these feelings only accentuates the fact that you are feeling better more of the time now than you used to feel. C.S. Lewis, noted British writer, has written this about these "interruptions":

> "The great thing, if one can, is to stop regarding all the unpleasant things as interruptions of one's "own" or "real" life. The truth is of course that what one calls the interruptions are precisely one's own life, the life God is sending one day by day." White. 170.

What you must always keep in perspective is that disruptions and uncomfortable feelings are just as much a part of your human existence as are joy, peace, and happiness. The unpleasant feelings just seem to hurt more now because you are vulnerable and more sensitive to pain than before your loss. What is lovely is that this can be a good quality if you use it to enhance your life and to bring about the growth of an empathic spirit. When you know pain, you become free to feel the pain of others around you and to be able to encourage them as you have been encouraged.

It is also lovely to realize that while pain may signal a condition of brokenness, pain is also a means of bringing you to a greater state of wholeness than before. Anne Morrow Lindbergh has written:

> I do not believe that sheer suffering teaches. If suffering alone taught, the entire world would be wise since everyone suffers. To suffering must be added mourning, understanding, patience, love, openness, and the willingness to remain vulnerable. All these and other factors combined, if the circumstances are right, *can* teach and *can* lead to rebirth. Lindburgh. 3.

As you maintain these attitudes, your pathway through suffering will be so much more tolerable and you will emerge at the end as a richer, wiser, more compassionate individual.

Along the Road

> I walked a mile with Pleasure,
> She chattered all the way,
> But left me none the wiser
> For all she had to say.
> I walked a mile with Sorrow,
> And ne'er a word said she;
> But, oh, the things
> I learned from her
> When Sorrow walked with me.
>
> Robert Browning. 34.

When Words Hurt . . .
Consider that which is lovely!

As a widow or widower, especially when your loss is a recent one, you tend to be extremely sensitive to things that others say or do that you might be able to ignore at another time in your life. However, because your emotions are raw and you are struggling every moment just to make it through another day without your loved one, one phrase, spoken by someone who has never experienced the pain that such a loss brings, can pierce the heart and cause the tears to flow.

Often the words are so inappropriate that they hurt tremendously, instead of giving you hope and encouragement. You have probably heard someone say, "Well, you are strong. You'll soon get over the loss," or how about, "He's in a better place now." A man once said the following words to me while I was mourning the death of my second husband: "He's been dead for three months now. You are just milking your grief." Most hurtful words are generally well intentioned to help the bereaved to accept the loss more easily. Words such as those spoken by that particular man apparently were spoken out of ignorance of the grieving process. Even though he, too, had lost a spouse many years before, perhaps he had denied his grief. It was obvious that the man did not know how to accept my expressions of grief, or perhaps my mourning created so much discomfort in the man that he had to be angry instead of acknowledging his own discomfort. Such words are often delivered thoughtlessly because people don't know how to deal with your pain, or perhaps because they can't deal with the subconscious fear of their own inevitable mortality. What they say may tend to make you feel that they think your loss is insignificant or unimportant, and often your hurt turns quickly to anger, and you respond with equally hurtful words that at another time you would never utter. If you could think logically about emotional experiences, you would be able to dismiss hurtful words as coming from the inexperienced or insensitive. But, emotional *reactions* differ significantly from intellectual *responses*. At this time in your life, you often find it very difficult to be rational.

How can such hurtful experiences ever have a lovely side to them? It seems ludicrous to even try to consider such. But, remember, your experiences are never wasted. If you are a Christian, trying to live the life that God has in mind for you, the hurts only serve to make you more dependent upon His love and His care for you. The hurts tend to make you more sensitive to how you, too, may have made the same mistakes before you understood the pain of bereavement. Hopefully, they teach you to be more empathic toward those you will encounter in the future who will experience similar pain.

The hurt that you feel can also reveal to you whether you are in need of growth in the area of forgiveness and grace. If you find yourself unable to forgive those who have hurt you, then God must want you to learn how to do that so that you will be made a much cleaner vessel for the work that He has in mind for you to yet accomplish in this world.

Yes, there is a lovely side to everything. You must learn to look for it because you must redeem the time that God has given to you to spread His love in this world.

> Forgive us our debts as we also have forgiven our debtors. And lead us not into temptation, but deliver us from the evil one.
> -Matthew 6:12-13 (NIV)

Powerful Words

> Our little words have power
> That we scarce can understand.
> They flow from us so freely
> Like water held in hand.
> They make their mark on others
> When we have come and gone.
> They bring happiness and laughter,
> Or they cause a dreadful wrong.
> Our words must be a measure
> Of our kindness and our love.
> For every word that's spoken
> Is heard by God above.
> Helen S. Peterson

When Your Nightmares Will Not Cease . . .
Consider that which is lovely!

There may be times during the grieving process that morning after morning you find yourself awakening from a dream that disturbs you. It may have been about something you and your loved one did together or perhaps about something that you wish you hadn't done. Sometimes these dreams are so confusing because other people play a part in them and you don't understand why. Perhaps other persons who also have died are a part of them, and it makes you wonder if you or another of your loved ones is going to die soon, too. If you study them closely they may seem to have a recurring theme. It may be that you feel powerless to help the one you loved. You may see them in danger and can't get to them. You may awaken feeling angry or afraid, or you may even feel rejected or abandoned.

Although dreams of your loved one often occur soon after your loss, as you are adjusting to the absence of that person from your life, they also may be more prevalent during times when you would have celebrated special occasions or when you have experienced an anniversary of the death. It is not unusual to feel a great deal of pain during these times since they were linked to special moments in your lives. In fact, the pain you may experience around the time of the anniversary of the death of your loved one may feel worse than that which you felt at the very beginning of your loss. This can be explained by the fact that when you first lost your loved one you were protected by a "blanket" of shock. Once that shock wears off, we have to face our losses with bare, raw emotions.

How could one look at these nocturnal experiences and consider them lovely when most of them *seem* to produce fear or sadness? Although the study of dreams is not an exact science, we do know that God used dreams in biblical times to enlighten His people. The same might be considered true with our dreams during bereavement. Modern-day psychologists tend to agree that dreams speak to us of those things that are just beneath the surface of our consciousness during our waking hours or of those issues with which we are struggling subconsciously. Because your emotional barricades are somewhat vulnerable during the time of bereavement, it may be that your brain is really trying to help you resolve some of those issues that never were resolved earlier in life. It may also be that your mind is helping you to deal with your losses by allowing you to accept the permanency of them. It may be that in your dreams you can express feelings that you might hesitate to express openly because of feelings of retribution or misunderstanding. Possibly your dreams offer new solutions or new perspectives to those situations that you encounter every day. If you are willing to examine the themes of the dreams, you may be able to face those feelings that seem to hinder your progress forward. In so doing, you may be able to rebuild your life so that you will face the future even more successfully than you did the past.

> (Lord) satisfy us in the morning with your unfailing love, that we may sing for joy and be glad all our days!
>
> -Psalm 90:14 (NIV)

Through the Darkness of the Night

Through the darkness of the night
My dreams have played relentlessly in my mind.
Shades of sorrow mingled with guilt
Have plagued my sleep like angry waves upon the sea wall.
Whether I twist or turn or try to run from them,
They follow as ghostly apparitions in the fog of life.
Why do they interrupt the peace that I long for?
What is the meaning of these sad and fearful memories?

As I awaken I long to remember. But alas,
Only the thoughts of my fears or anger encompass me.
I search for the meaning amidst my tattered memories.
Ah, Yes. Now I understand.
I am saddened by mistakes I have made.
I regret things left undone.
I do not want to release the love I knew,
As though to keep it would correct the past.
I do not want to be alone to face life by myself
In an uncertain world.

Yet, somehow I know I have done as well as I could.
I know I am strong and able to surge ahead.
The pathway is uncertain. But so it was before.

Pain

I am alone now. But even then my decisions were my own.
I am afraid. But fear has always been a part of life.
With God's help I have conquered in the past.
With His help I will continue to conquer.
I will go on and become more of whom God wants me to be.
I will live through the disturbing nights
Until I see the joyful light of day.

Helen S. Peterson

When Nighttime Brings No Solace from the Pain . . .
Consider that which is lovely!

Although it doesn't happen every night, there are some nights when we just can't sleep. One night, when I went to bed exhausted at nine thirty in the evening, I thought that I would fall asleep immediately. At four thirty in the morning, after lying quietly for almost seven hours, awake and with my mind mulling over thoughts of when my spouse was with me, or of things we had done together, or of those things that I still had to do to "normalize" my life again, I finally got up and went to the kitchen where I devoured a large glass of warm milk and two cookies. I went back to bed and finally slept for three hours until I was awakened by the telephone. What a night. I wondered if it would ever end. My heart was heavy, I was exhausted, and I felt as though the terrible pain would never end.

No doubt you have had similar experiences. In the darkness, there seems to be so much less hope. You desperately need the rest to allow your chaotic thoughts to reorganize in order for you to regain health, but it seems that even God has deserted you in those dark hours of the night. The pain is not always severe, but the ache still remains and the void is always there.

It is not a lovely thing to lie awake all night, but the important thing to remember when sleep will not come is that it is still important to get rest for the body. By lying still and just allowing your muscles to relax, your body has a chance to rejuvenate itself. Of course, you may be tempted to arise and become interested in something that will take your mind from the ever-cycling thoughts that interfere with your sleep. However, if you examine what is happening, you may find that these sleepless times are really blessings for they are times of growth and change. While it is not comfortable to ruminate over your losses, at times such rumination allows your brain to process them so that they become real. Often during your days you are distracted by other activities, and you seldom find the time to reflect and process what has occurred in your life. In time, as your brain and your emotions can accept that the loss is permanent, generally you will not experience such disturbing or sleepless times. But for now, change from within is what you need to help you to grow and to become the new individual that you are becoming. If you are willing to live patiently through this dark season of painful growth, one day you will see the light of the sunshine after a good night's sleep.

If you remember King David of Old Testament days, he was troubled with not being able to sleep because of grief in his life. Here is what he said to God:

> You kept my eyes from closing;
> I was too troubled to speak.
> I thought about the former days,
> the years of long ago;
> I remembered my songs in the night.
> My heart mused and my spirit inquired:
> "Will the Lord reject us forever?
> Will he never show his favor again?"
>
> -Psalm 77:4–7 (NIV)

Sometimes you may feel as though God will not show his favor upon you again. In the darkness you may sometimes feel as though God has deserted you and will not return to help you. However, that is far from the truth. God never leaves us. He is there even in the dark, sleepless night, and He will reveal himself when you are ready to accept his blessings.

Our Journey through Life

Pain and confusion abound in this life,
Some sparkles of joy amidst struggle and strife.
How do we gain some peace deep within?
When will night end and the daylight begin?

Life's pages were blank when the journey began.
A gift that was precious awaited our pen.
The moments came, and the years now have gone.
Seems like yesterday when we'd started for home.

We found our true love and lived happily on.
But now that is over. From the earth he is gone.
No peace from the pain as the darkness descends,
No rest for our brains as the night never ends.

Yet in the midst of our grief and the pain that we feel,
Deep down in our hearts we are beginning to heal.
We can't see the changes, the way isn't clear.
The darkness lingers on, forever we fear.

One morn, to our surprise and grateful delight,
The darkness recedes and the sun shines so bright.
Our sleepless nights end as day breaks anew,
Though pain held us captive, our spirits still grew.

Now on a new road we move on ahead.
After facing the night we have nothing to dread.
Life's pages were blank when the journey began.
Now the gift that is precious awaits our new pen.

Helen S. Peterson

Coping with the Anniversary Date . . .
Consider that which is lovely!

Feelings of sadness and sorrow often emerge at the time of the anniversary of a loved one's death. The questions that have been tucked away once again work themselves to the foreground of consciousness. "Why did my loved one have to die so soon?" "Will I have to live the rest of my life without having someone to love or someone who loves me?" "Could I have done anything differently to prolong life?" "Why don't others feel as sad as I do?" "Do they even care?"

All of these questions are normal. As stated before, there are really no answers to them. Perhaps during this time of grief and mourning you have come to some answers, but possibly even the answers you have found are inadequate. They are simply ways you have learned to cope with the pain of your loss. It is hard to accept, but now you must find a way to live a new "normal" life. Death is final. It is hard for us to accept because deep within us is the desire to go on living life here on this earth. It is hard for us to accept because it reminds us that one day, we too, will die.

So, what is lovely about going through the pain of an anniversary? Is there really anything to be gained? First, you can't avoid it, and you can't forget it because the brain has it locked into memory. Second, remember that God did not intend for us to die, and therefore he did not intend for us to experience grief. In his foreknowledge of human behavior, though, God designed the experiences of grief and mourning for a reason. He knew the course that people need to take in order to heal. Perhaps the pain that comes with experiencing these memorable times can bring a new appreciation of your own life. Perhaps these are times to make changes for the good. Perhaps, with each passing special date, you can make a special effort to let go of some of the hurts and remember only the wonderful events and attributes associated with your deceased loved one. Perhaps these will be times you may come to a new appreciation of the differences in people. You might use the occurrences of the anniversaries as steppingstones to taking action against some of the atrocious causes of death such as drunken drivers, cancers, homicides, or even just poor living habits such as lack of exercise or poor nutrition. All these are things you can do to turn the suffering into something meaningful and lovely.

While grief and mourning are not pleasant, and while persons who have not grieved or mourned often do not understand your feelings, you do not have to lose joy or peace in the process. Joy comes from knowing that you had the opportunity to have someone of great value in your life. Joy comes from remembering the wonderful experiences or qualities of that person. And, in the case of those who believe in an afterlife with God, joy comes from believing that someday you will be reunited with the one you loved so dearly. Peace comes from knowing that there really is a God who cares about you and who will hold your hand as you travel this difficult path at this time.

The Serenity Prayer

God grant me the serenity to accept
The things I cannot change;
Courage to change the things I can;
And wisdom to know the difference.
Living one day at a time;
Enjoying one moment at a time;
Accepting hardships as the pathway to peace;
Taking as He did, this sinful world as it is,
Not as I would have it;
Trusting that He will make all things right
If I surrender to His Will;
That I may be reasonably happy in this life
And supremely happy with Him
Forever in the next.

Attributed to Reinhold
Niebuhr from 1937 on

When You Crave a Change . . .
Consider that which is lovely!

It is so easy to become reclusive when you are experiencing grief. All you have to do is nothing. That's it. You stay at home where it is safe, or you attend your job at the office but remain withdrawn from those around you. After all, if you are at home, no one can see your inertia, and when you are at the office, you can concentrate on your job and for a short while delay the feelings you experience. Yet, you crave change. You crave that social contact you may have had long before the death of your loved one. You crave meaningful activity in your life, but you just can't bring yourself to believe it will ever be there again.

Consider it lovely that we are all created with that desire for social interaction and meaningful engagement. Consider it lovely that we do not like isolation or pain. Consider it lovely that when you use your logic instead of relying on feelings, you can change. That's right. We all have the power within to make choices. It is, however, a power of the intellect and not of the feelings. You can make the choice to interact meaningfully with others. You can make the choice to share your feelings with those whom you know will understand. You can make the choice to become actively involved with life again.

You may ask, "But how do I do that?" There is a saying that is often carelessly uttered by carefree young people but which certainly applies here: "Just do it." You may not feel like going to a wedding, a church service, out to eat for dinner, or to a play or concert. But, if you just do it anyway, by making the effort you will find new strength of which you were unaware. Sometimes it helps to "just do it" with a close friend or relative, but you really cannot depend on others to give you the strength to begin life anew.

It will be terribly hard at first. You will desire to be back in your safety zone. You may second-guess yourself and ask: "Why am I here doing this?" Yet as you develop a new awareness of the world around you that is still alive, you will gradually lose that need for safety. At some point you may decide to begin a new hobby such as learning to dance, studying another language, or becoming a photographer. You will have to enroll in classes in order to learn those things. You may decide to take a cruise or a land tour somewhere you had always wished to go. It will be so hard. You will feel all alone, even in the group. But, eventually you will develop a sense of pride in the fact that you are trying. Remember, if you never try, you will never know if you would have succeeded. Further, as you make the tough choice to enter into life again, you will find that there are lots of people who have felt just as you do now. They have had to find their way back to life, and maybe they are doing exactly the same things you are doing. As you interact, you gain new strength and comfort that others do understand and can give you encouragement as you forge ahead into the future.

Consider this: if God chose to keep you here instead of your loved one, then He has something that He wants for you to do in this world. He wants you to join Him in whatever it is that He is already doing. That is a lovely thought. What could be more wonderful than joining with God in His plans to redeem the creatures of this world? Consider it all lovely that you are able to change your way of living and thinking in order to fulfill that important mission.

> "Getting over a painful experience is much like crossing monkey bars.
> You have to let go at some point in order to move forward."
>
> Anonymous

God,

I say that I want a change in my life, yet I am so resistant toward the changes that have happened already. I don't like the inertia or the listlessness, but I am afraid to move out of that circle of safety. I want to make new friends and do new things, but when I do, I feel so strange making the change without the security that my loved one offered. I know that many things in my life have changed, and I surely don't like many of the changes. Is this the plan you have for me? If you want me to change again, you will have to help me. I am afraid to do it by myself. Nevertheless, I trust that you know what is best for me. I am willing to do what you want me to do. Amen.

CONFUSION

When Confusion Abounds . . .
Consider that which is lovely!

    There are so many things to do to get your life back into some semblance of order. Even if you are the one who took care of all the business matters, there are still forms to fill out, a will to probate, or maybe property names to change. This whole process takes your time and energy when you would rather be getting on with life and not hurting so much. If you had not been the one in the relationship who took care of most of the business matters, the cars, the house, the insurance, and all that goes along with living, you may feel overwhelmed and totally confused. My goodness, all the information might be on some computer, but you don't know the slightest bit about how to use it. How frustrating that is! Some days you may become angry that now you are being forced to assume responsibility for that which you never had to before. You have to learn things you really don't want to learn. Some days you may feel that you do not even know where to begin to make things less chaotic or confusing for yourself. You may feel as though you are lost in the forest at night and will never again see the light of day.

    Then, there is that whole other matter of disposing of the loved ones belongings—clothing, personal articles, collections, books, tools or craft supplies, and the like. Each time you attempt to think about it you become so filled with nostalgia or sorrow or loneliness that you just can't bear to begin or to continue the tasks. Confusion abounds. Just how can that ever have a lovely side?

    Whenever growth has occurred in your life, whether it was when you were getting your new teeth as an infant, mending a broken bone as a child, going to school for the first time, or taking your driver's license test, there was some pain and confusion. You had to adapt to each of these changes until you felt the pain go away. Eventually, the growth occurred, the pain disappeared, and you were better for it.

    The growth that happens when you lose a loved one and are forced to learn new responsibilities can continue to be painful if you refuse to deal with the confusion or pain. You can stop feeling the pain and confusion *as you make the efforts* to learn and to grow in those areas. This growth process can then provide a new sense of confidence in what you are able to accomplish all by yourself. As you painfully work through one part of the puzzle at a time, you begin to look at the picture as it takes on a whole new meaning. You develop a sense of pride in accomplishing that which you never before thought you could accomplish. And you gain confidence from the fact that you really do have within you hidden skills and talents that never were revealed because you did not have to use them.

The lovely part of all of this confusion and chaos is that it forces you to grow in order to get rid of the tension and pain that the confusion produces. It is a means to understanding that you are capable of far more than you had ever realized, and it is the beginning of a new way of thinking, behaving, and dreaming for the future.

"I can do everything through him who gives me strength."
-Philippians 4:13 (NIV)

Going On, Going On!

It has been said "When life gives you lemons,
Make lemonade!"
I say, when life passes you by,
"Join the parade!"
When life is like a drab, old toy,
Don't let sorrow rob your joy!
When life seems rainy and bleak for you,
Raise your 'brella and whistle a tune!
When life is boring, as it sometimes will be,
Turn your ear to nature's symphony!
When life seems hopeless and without much joy,
Get ready to work and your talents employ!
When the day is long and the nights are, too,
Give of yourself—to many or few!
Don't let the struggles of life overwhelm!
You are on God's ship, and He's at the helm!

Helen S. Peterson

When You Feel Really Mixed Up . . .
                          Consider that which is lovely!

You have lost a loved one. Perhaps you have cared for that person while they were ill for one or two years, or maybe for ten or fifteen years. You are feeling relieved that your days of being a caretaker are finally over. Yet you feel tremendous guilt because you feel such relief. You are angry because you wonder how God could have allowed that person to live so long under duress. You are angry because so many years of your life have been given away to another person. You are angry because many times you were tired and felt as though you could not go on, but you had to because no one else was there to do the job. You had no other choice. You are so mixed up because of your loss, because of your anger, because of your sense of relief, and because now you don't know what to do with the time that used to be concentrated on taking care of your loved one.

Those certainly are a myriad of feelings with which to cope, but take heart. When you experience those feelings, rest assured that you are not alone. Many others have lived through the same feelings. They are normal when you have lived through anticipatory grief for a prolonged period as the primary caregiver. In fact, you may have been living in anticipatory grief for so long that now you can't distinguish it from the grief you presently feel.

What could possibly be lovely about your situation? Think about this. You have a mission on this earth. Part of that mission, which you did not ask for or desire, was to care for an ailing loved one. You have successfully seen that loved one through to his or her death. That part of your mission is now fulfilled, and God is pleased with how you managed. He has seen all of your struggles and is pleased that now you are free to complete another part of your mission in life. How wonderful. It may not seem so wonderful at this very moment, but look at your freedom from a new vantage. You know how to be a caretaker. You know how to persist when you feel as though you can't go on another moment. You have learned that you are not perfect, but that it is okay. Now you are learning that it is okay to feel great relief. You are not disrespecting your loved one. God has got some other things for you to do so you may use your talents and abilities in other ways.

Long ago God promised that He would "Restore the years the locusts have eaten" Joel 2:25 (NIV). A plague of locusts was sent to the land of Egypt as a sign to Pharaoh that God would release the nation of Israel from his control.

Confusion

When the locusts swarmed the land, they stripped all the vegetation totally bare. They did not spare the Israelites even though God was working to free them from the rule of the Egyptian Pharaoh. At times you have felt as though your work as a caregiver stripped you bare. With the death of your loved one, you feel even more stripped than before. The promise is meant for you today as well as for those ancient Israelites. Of course, you have feelings of anger, sadness, fear, relief, and guilt. These feelings will subside with time. Of course, you are tired and possibly not in very good physical condition from the stress of it all. Perhaps you even feel as though your life has been wasted. You may feel as though what you have done during this time of your life has been meaningless. Never fear, God has been watching! Even when no one else is aware of what you have given up, God knows. He said He would restore the years that the locusts have eaten away Joel 2:25 (NIV). God will restore the life that you have given away. He will restore you to better life than ever before. God is able to fill your remaining years with rich experiences that you never dreamed possible.

You gave of yourself and delayed your own gratification for the good of your loved one. God says in John 15:13 (KJV) that: "There is no greater love than this that a man lay down his life for his friend." You have done that and God is well pleased with you.

Now you are free to do some of the things that are uniquely you. You can wear the kinds of clothes that you want to wear. You can travel to places to which you would like to travel. You can go to sleep when you want and get up when you want. You can use your car the way you want. You can even have the kind of car you may want! You can give away the things that you want to give away. You can arrange your furniture the way you want it. You can even get rid of some of what you don't like and get what you do like.

You are free to visit your friends when you are able to do so. You are free to eat when and what you want. You do not have to cook any meals for anyone except when you wish to do so. You can spend your money wisely, but as you wish to spend it. You can live without fear of recrimination for the things you do or don't do.

You are free to be the person that God wants you to be at this time. You have been living the life that He has preordained for you as you have come through the years. But now there is another life. There is a life in which you can come and go as you desire, as long as it is within God's perfect will.

Be assured that this new freedom may sometimes get you into trouble. At times you will make poor decisions or use your freedom without real consideration for the consequences. But know that eventually, as long as you desire God's will for your life, you will fulfill the rest of the mission that He has for you on this earth. And, you will be blessed in doing so.

WASTED TIME

Life is so precarious...
Yet we live so unaware
That each moment is a precious one,
With not a second to spare.

Sometimes we do not think
Of the treasure we are given.
We have not a moment to waste
As we move our life toward heaven.

Each moment is a precious gem
Shining through our day.
We must guard our gems so carefully,
Losing none along the way.

You have spent some precious gems
Caring for one you love.
God has seen your sacrifice
Watching you from above.

When you have come to end of your days
And your gems...they are all gone
You can say with pride you have
Spent them well and now your life is done!

Helen S. Peterson

No Personal Time to Think . . .
Consider that which is lovely!

Going through the grieving process requires you to search quietly for new meanings for your life. Because grief feels so awful, and because there are so many people who think they know what is the best thing for you to do, they often inundate your life very soon after you have experienced your loss. Mostly, they do this out of love for you. Some do it because they have not completed their own grief process and they need to fill the gap in their own lives. Sometimes it is out of sheer ignorance or inquisitiveness. At times their presence or advice or questions can seem overwhelming and even suffocating. I remember one man asked me the question, "Will you be able to keep your house?" I am not sure why he asked, but it took me by surprise because I had not even gotten to the point where I was able to think about such things. I was simply dealing with the immediate loss and did not need to consider another loss. He was ignorant of how his question may have affected me. (I did not have to leave my house, and in fact, at this time still live in it!)

Unfortunately, sometimes you allow people entrance into your life because you really do not know who you are or because you really do not want to endure the pain that comes with loss by yourself. Yet, the very presence of too many persons wanting too much from you can be very exhausting. It is during times such as these that you frequently may feel as though you really have no time to explore your grief and to remold your life to the new circumstances that now surround you. At times you might like to scream out "Please, leave me alone and let me grieve in the manner that I think is best for me."

If you are one who has experienced this overwhelming display of care or concern, think about what is really going on around you. Others have also lost your loved one. You may not be fully aware of that thought at the moment, but it is true. In that case, it is lovely that others want to gather around you to console you but also to gain solace for themselves. It is lovely that there are friends and acquaintances who think it important to give you as much support as possible. It is lovely that there may be some with whom you may be able to share, at a later date, just because of the concern they have expressed at this time. And, it is lovely that because of having people surround you, you may become more aware of some of the wonderful things that your loved one did or said of which you were not aware.

If you do experience this overwhelming display of compassion, it is perfectly all right for you to express your need for time to be alone quietly. Often you can count upon a close friend to speak for you if you feel as though you are being ungrateful or rude.

Dear Father,

If I could only know what to expect, then maybe I could make better decisions. I am so tired of having to entertain the well-wishers in my life. They keep giving me advice about things I don't want to think about right now. It is so perplexing to not know which way to go and which decision to make. Right now my brain feels as though I am in a mental daze. I am living in a fog. I hate this feeling. Can't you please help me? Won't you do something to make it clearer for me? Amen.

A Look into the Future

If the future we could see
How difficult our lives might be.
When wishing for a future sight,
We really want what's good and right.
Yet we know life's not that way,
For darkness always follows day.

If the future we could see
How unhappy we might be.
Though joy and gladness will be there,
So will times of dark despair.
And, when all is said and done,
We can't prepare for either one.

We must learn to live today,
And do our best in work and play.
Tomorrow will come in its own time,
Today we've all got mountains to climb.
The future holds its own allure.
We'll enter it when today is no more.

Helen S. Peterson

Thanks for the Advice, but . . .
Consider that which is lovely!

There are times when you must be alone to process your thoughts and to deal with the loss that you have experienced. Yet, loving friends and relatives just seem to overtake your life. They think you need company so that you won't get depressed or morose, or they give advice as to how you should live your life in the future. Although they mean well, many have not been where you are in your life situation, and they really don't understand how tired you get or how you need a quiet and calm environment in which to think, to cry, and to heal. Many could never do the things you are capable of doing around your home, and so they make suggestions as to how you should manage. But, you are not ready to make the changes they suggest. Your home is your refuge— the place where you find comfort and security. To think of uprooting or changing your living circumstances, if you really don't need to do so, completely upsets you. Yet, as much as you tell them, they keep on giving their "free advice" without really hearing you. What a painful situation it creates. You are trying to make the myriad of adjustments needed to live without the one you loved, and then they suggest even more drastic adjustments.

What is lovely about this situation is that you can grow from it. Decide what is best for you right now, and just keep your resolve. Perhaps this is not a mode that you are used to, but it is a wonderful skill to have in order to deal with the affairs of everyday life out in the precarious world of business. Be assertive. Speak up kindly, and let your advisors know you appreciate their efforts but you are not ready to make the changes they suggest. You may always change your decisions as time goes by, but that is your choice and you will make it when you are ready to make it, not when others think you should make it. The sense of independence that results from making a few simple decisions not to change before you are ready to do so is remarkable. It provides you with a sense of control at a time when you feel as though life has been out of control.

Further, as you keep your resolve to do the things that are important for your healthy life, you will learn which things are good for you and which you wish to discard. Those discarded may be ones that you did because you loved your spouse and did not want to deprive him or her of the joy of having things that way. Those kept or changed may be the ones that lead you to a new sense of creativity and independence in your new life ahead. Life is not static. Life is ever changing. Give yourself permission to listen to yourself and to do the things that you believe are best for you. As you learn to change appropriately, using the wisdom imparted from God through your life experiences, you will find a new sense of joy in who you are as an individual.

Remember, if you consult God first, listen to His word, follow the leading of His spirit speaking to you through your thoughts, and if you feel a sense of peace inside, then you can consult those well-meaning loved ones in your life. God will never lead you astray. He knows the plans He has for you. Wait for Him.

> "Have you ever come on anything quite like this extravagant generosity of God, this deep, deep wisdom? It's way over our heads. We'll never figure it out."
>
> -Romans 11:33 (MSG)

God,

Sometimes I feel so overwhelmed with all of the company in my life.
I hate to be alone, but I also need to spend quiet time with you . . .
thinking . . . praying . . . and reassessing who I am.
Help me to let them know kindly what MY needs are
so that they can allow me to grow through this painful time
in the manner that I need to grow . . . how You want me to grow.
Give me the wisdom to know what things need to be changed and
what I need to leave alone for the moment.
Give me the strength to listen and
yet to be able to say "no" in a quiet, firm and loving manner
when all kinds of advice comes my way.
Give me the ability to make the right decisions in the proper time
so that I will become stronger, wiser
and more of whom you have designed me to be.
I want to grow through my experiences in life . . .
whether they be sad or glad.
I thank you for your presence in my life today.
I will listen to your voice and obey. Amen.

Living Life as a Caterpillar . . .
Consider that which is lovely!

There are times while you are grieving your loss when you may feel as though you are living life as a caterpillar. Things just keep moving at their normal pace all around you, but there you are, creeping along from leaf to leaf looking for something of value in life. All you want to do is to get inside a safe cocoon and hide. Of course, you don't really know what happens inside the cocoon, but it seems as though it would be better than this aimless feeling of being lost and confused.

Sometimes this happens when you find yourself left to sort through business or personal matters with which you are not familiar. What was of value to your spouse: jewelry, clothing, tools, books, papers, cards, pictures, collections, and so forth may not have that same value to you. Yet, you are the one who must make the important decisions of what to do with them. Some of it is easy because you can give them to others who might like them as mementos of that person. However, nostalgia grabs at your heart because you do not want to depart with those things that your loved one treasured or felt were necessary in life. At the same time, you know that you will not use these belongings or even find them of interest. Guilt plagues your spirit because disposing of those things may feel as though you are disposing of your loved one's life. In some ways it is as though you are disposing of a life. However, it is really more appropriate to think of your endeavors as only putting closure to your loved one's life here on earth.

Many times it is simply a practical matter of getting rid of things that are no longer useful, but at other times it is a matter of disposing of those things that will no longer fit into a smaller location or into your new life. Often the overwhelming task of going through that "stuff" brings pain to your heart and tears to your eyes. And then, you begin to wonder why these things were so valuable when what really mattered was the life that once was attached to them.

Sometimes these feelings occur when well-meaning loved ones and friends are expecting you to be normal again. They just keep doing everything in their power to make things that way. They come in and start to sort through things before you are ready to let go of them, or they begin to tell you how you "need" to do this or that. Sometimes these feelings happen just because you are devoid of energy from the heaviness of grief, yet everyone around tells you that it is time for you to get going again.

How can you even think of anything lovely when life is askew and missing the focus that once it had? Consider the life of a lovely butterfly. From a nondescript worm in a cocoon, there eventually emerges a thing of beauty. But, this transformation only comes after crawling through a portion of life as a caterpillar, eating holes in leaves, getting wrapped up in an ugly cocoon, and then struggling for what must seem to be an interminable amount of time before emerging. You have little idea of what the change process feels like to a caterpillar, but you surely don't enjoy it in you. We are told by scientists that unless that butterfly struggles as it begins to emerge from the cocoon, it will have no strength to unfold its wings. Only after struggling is it able to spread its wings in the sunshine to dry and then eventually fly off as a creature of beauty.

As you barely creep through the early days of grieving you suddenly find yourself wrapped up in your "cocoon" of grief. You stay there for a while as you grow. Finally as you struggle with the affairs of life, you emerge as a new creature. Gradually, you unfold your wings and let them dry in the sun. You can't see it immediately, but you have become more beautiful than you have ever been before. At some point you have the hope that you will be able to "spread your wings" and take flight into a new and adventuresome life ahead. That is the lovely part of living through the struggle of metamorphosis. There is an old saying that says something to the effect that there is no gain without any pain. Perhaps you have found that to be true even at this point in your journey to a new life.

> "Those who hope in the Lord will renew their strength. They will soar on wings like eagles; they will run and not grow weary; they will walk and not be faint."
>
> -Isaiah 40:31 (NIV)

God,

This day has been like a nightmare. The issues of life through which I must sort are so foreign to me. I know that once they carried purpose, and I try to remember that my task is to find things of value amidst the chaos. But sometimes it is so hard, and it seems so fruitless. If you would, I ask for you to give me the courage to face these tasks that must be done. I ask for wisdom to make correct decisions. I thank you for those who give me encouragement and support as I know it is just as hard for them to help me as it is for me to keep going on. I am struggling to regain balance. Please renew my strength until I emerge into a new life. Amen.

Life as a Patchwork Quilt . . .
Consider that which is lovely!

    Patchwork quilts were very popular years ago. They were works of art created out of the need of people to keep warm. When you look at the parts of an old patchwork quilt, it may seem that it is made of rags or disjointed pieces. But, when laundered, ironed smooth, and used for the purpose for which they were created, patchwork quilts can become the most beautiful, treasured, and comfortable possessions you have. Memories come alive when you view the seemingly disjointed and uncoordinated pieces. Feelings of affection arise when you think about the one or ones who tirelessly put together these precious creations. And there arises a sense of comfort and security in the joy of wrapping yourself in one of these lovely creations.

    Sometimes your life seems to be put together like a patchwork quilt. This is particularly true when you experience the loss of something or someone dear or precious to you. As time goes by, your life feels as though it is simply "sewn" together in discordant parts. You may wonder if you will ever see a pattern that is lovely or normal again. Until the pattern is complete or until you see it from afar, you don't really know the beauty that is being created with all the jumbled parts of your life.

    Is there really anything lovely about this ugly piece of patchwork that you call your life? The pieces of your "patchwork quilt" life may consist of loneliness, regret, guilt, sadness, questioning, anger, brokenness, feelings of abandonment, fear of the future, confusion, hurt, and even a sense of hopelessness. There are some dirty, torn, uneven pieces in the quilt. But, you can't make your life over. You add to your life; you don't take away from it. When you add friendships, joys, wholeness, feelings of accomplishment, excitement for what the future may hold, held together with great hope, then the beautiful pieces in that quilt outshine the old ones that have lost their luster. The quilt takes on a whole new look and meaning.

    Just wait and keep on "patching." When your life seems like a patchwork quilt, trust that God, the Creator, is making it into a beautiful, comfortable, unique, and very special piece of art that you will appreciate and that others will see as beautiful, comfortable and treasured. When you view your life from "down underneath" it may seem as though it is a hodgepodge of experiences, with nothing to hold them together or to give them meaning. But, once you are on the "top side" of your life again, you will be able to see the loveliness that develops as a result of adding new experiences and gaining new skills. Seeing the beauty that has come from your times of disappointments and struggles, you will regain a feeling of wholeness and a sense of who you really are in the eyes of your loving God.

Even though the threads may look tangled and uneven from the backside, when you add the padding and finish the underside, the quilt of your life becomes more useful than ever before. The side that presents the beauty becomes the side that others can see and experience. Your life will become not only a lovely creation for the world to enjoy, but your life will be more useful in the kingdom of God because of the many parts that have become melded together.

Your Life Is a Patchwork Quilt

> To realize the value of that one kind word you spoke,
> Ask the one who had given up hope when you came along.
> To realize the value of tears which have been shed,
> Ask the one with whom you cried as they struggled with grief.
> To realize the value of kindness,
> Ask the one to whom you gave your gloves in the winter storm.
> To realize the value of a moment in time,
> Ask the one with whom you sat as their loved one left this earth.
> To realize the value of a simple smile and loving arms,
> Ask the little child whom you comforted.
> To realize the value of your life on this earth,
> Just ask those who love you in spite of yourself.
> Your life may be only a patchwork quilt,
> But that quilt is a symbol of strength, comfort, love and care.
> Just ask me . . . I will tell you so.

Helen S. Peterson

Emotional Endoscopy . . .

Consider that which is lovely!

Do you sometimes feel as though you are now living in a daze and just don't seem to deal with life the way that you used to when your loved one was alive? I liken it to when the gastroenterologist is about to do an endoscopic procedure. He gives you a little bit of something to make you feel *really* drowsy. You are just awake enough to cooperate but not awake enough to interfere. When the doctor is inserting the tube into you, sometimes you feel as though you want to gag, which is something like how you feel when you are lonesome or by yourself in a crowd. But, once the tube is down your throat successfully, you are generally in such a daze that you can't feel a thing that is going on. The doctor then examines the inside of you so that later he can prescribe medication or make changes if necessary.

This thing we call grief can be the protective "pill" that keeps us functioning while going through what might be called "emotional endoscopy." The good part is that while you have the discomfort of knowing that something is going on inside, you are not totally aware of everything that is happening. Our spiritual doctor, God, continues to monitor what is happening both inside and outside, even when you are not aware of it. In the meantime, you keep adjusting to changes while life goes on around you. When you finally awaken from your pain, you find that many changes have happened almost without your knowing they were taking place.

Our Creator didn't intend for us to have to endure the awful feelings that go along with loss. In fact, He created us not to die. But in His wisdom and knowing what He already knew about the humans He had created, He did endow us with the ability to self-protect and to manage to overcome that pain. Yes, it sometimes seems as though you are just living a bad dream and that you will awaken and find that what you are experiencing is not real. It is truly wonderful to know that you have a God who looked far enough ahead to provide you with the tools that will once again bring you to back to your life, fully awake, fully aware, more mature, and ready to face the future with joy and great peace.

> "Hear, O Lord, and answer me, for I am poor and needy. Guard my life, for I am devoted to you. You are my God. Save your servant who trusts in you. Have mercy on me, O Lord, for I call to you all day long. Bring joy to your servant, for to you, O Lord, I lift up my soul. You are forgiving and good, O Lord, abounding in love to all who call to you."
> -Psalm 86:1–5 (NIV)

The "Don't Quit" Poem

When things go wrong, as they sometimes will,
When the road you're trudging seems all uphill,
When the funds are low and the debts are high,
And you want to smile, but you have to sigh,
When care is pressing you down a bit,
Rest, if you must, but don't you quit.
Life is queer with its twists and turns,
As every one of us sometimes learns,
And many a failure turns about,
When he might have won had he stuck it out;
Don't give up though the pace seems slow—
You may succeed with another blow.
Often the goal is nearer than
It seems to a faint and faltering man.
Often the struggler has given up,
When he might have captured the victor's cup;
And he learned too late when the night slipped down,
How close he was to the golden crown.
Success is failure turned inside out—
The silver tint of the clouds of doubt,
And you never can tell how close you are,
It may be near when it seems so far,
So stick to the fight when you're hardest hit—
It's when things seem worst that you must not quit.

Author unknown

Everything Has Changed . . .
Consider that which is lovely!

You hear *"all"* the other widows or widowers saying it: "Everything is different now," "Everything has changed," or "Things are not the same anymore without. . . ." Yes, lots of things have changed. Your marital status has changed. A source of companionship has changed. Perhaps even the person who has to deal with the business affairs of life has changed.

Having to change what you do and the way you do it is sometimes scary because human beings like consistency and balance. You prefer to remain comfortably nestled in your little groove and don't like being disturbed. God has created everything in His universe with a need for consistency and balance. He also has created you with the ability to grow through change. Making certain decisions by yourself can be frightening if you haven't been accustomed to making those kinds of decisions before the loss of your loved one. Being totally responsible for your home, your car, your belongings, and your money may shake your confidence at first. Allowing others to fill your life with their love for you may be foreign and frightening.

Look realistically at how much things have changed. Choose to view the situation with a clear mind rather than through an emotional haze. There is a witty legend that says, "It is awfully difficult to be optimistic if your optics are misty." So clean your optics and let's look at what has changed.

First, you have lived *all* your life with change. The fact is, that change happens all around and within you, every day that you live, and even when you die. From the time you were forming in your mother's womb until this very moment, you have been coping with change. For the most part you have been successful. You already have lots of experience coping with or accepting change. You can rely on inner strength that you have developed all along, but perhaps you had not used in the situations you are now encountering.

Second, not *everything* in your life has changed. You still eat, sleep, breathe, and carry on daily life activities in much the same way as you always did. You haven't suddenly forgotten all the skills that you had before you became widowed. You still have friends or relatives who care about you. And, you still have the faith inside of you that has provided hope for better times ahead in life. Chances are, you needed help when you were first learning to walk or to ride a bike or to drive a car. So what is different now? At times we have all needed help to learn new skills.

Third, just because you don't have your spouse with whom to do things, doesn't mean that suddenly you must stop doing. That is the beauty of being forced to change. You have the opportunity to meet lots of new people with new perspectives in new situations, doing things you have never have done before. What could be better for your spiritual and emotional growth?

Let's look at the lovely side to changing. Change is not your enemy. *Fear* of change is your enemy. Change can be the impetus to be remade and revitalized. Change can be God's way of helping you to become even more of the person He created you to be. Change can be challenging, exciting, and the path to a renewed life. Consider that which is lovely and embrace it again. Remember, if nothing ever changed, there would be no butterflies.

> "The happiest of people don't necessarily have the best of everything, they just make the best of everything they have."
>
> -Source Unknown

> "The truth is that our finest moments are most likely to occur when we are feeling deeply uncomfortable, unhappy, or unfulfilled. For it is only in such moments, propelled by our discomfort, that we are likely to step out of our ruts and start searching for different ways or truer answers." Peck. 89.

Some Times You Have to Walk Away

> Life is sometimes very drear.
> Uncertainty here below
> Often makes you cringe with fear
> And causes tears to flow.
>
> Oftentimes you dread the day;
> Within you, fear just grows.
> But at times, you have to walk away
> To learn where the pathway goes.
>
> And even though the path is strewn
> With obstacles along the way,

Confusion

Never think you are alone
For those who love you always stay.

To many you've brought hope anew
In ways you'll never know.
They want to walk the way with you
As down the path you go.

So share with them your need today,
Never fear that you impose.
Because sometimes, you have to walk a way
To know that God's great love still flows.

Helen S. Peterson

Afraid You Are Losing Your Mind . . .
Consider that which is lovely!

Sometimes, when you are grieving, it may seem as though you can't deal with the pain or the loss. You may feel that you are just going to "lose your mind." Sometimes, it is difficult to talk to people about your feelings of loss because they have gone on with their lives and seem to expect you to do the same. Further, you don't want others to know how overwhelmed you are at times, perhaps weeping and feeling depressed and despondent. People often unwittingly express false expectations that you feel obliged to fulfill. Sometimes when they see you out in public, they comment that you are doing so well or that you seem to be so strong or even that you seem to be healing very quickly. In an effort not to burden them or to let them down, you frequently do not tell them of the times spent alone grieving deeply, feeling deserted or isolated from the world. It is in those times that you feel so out of control emotionally and fear that you may, indeed, be "losing your mind.

Because the loss is so great, often you yearn to see or touch or hear that loved one just one more time. Not having them with you anymore sometimes brings such pain that you actually experience it physically. Sometimes your head aches or your bones seem to groan. At other times it seems as though your heart would stop beating because of the great physical pain. There have been many times when you believe that your loved one has actually come back to you. They may appear to be younger or healthier or just slightly different from when they left you, but nevertheless, you have seen them. These experiences comfort you, but at the same time you hesitate to tell anyone about them in case they think you are just a little bit unstable and perhaps hallucinating.

Psychiatrists generally do tell us that these experiences are, indeed, hallucinations or figments of our imagination that occur because we want our loved ones so desperately. Perhaps that is so. I prefer a different, far less orthodox explanation for these occurrences. For those who believe in God, and know His word to be true, there can be another explanation. God is the God of comfort. He is a God who grieves when we grieve, and He is a God who does not want His children to suffer unnecessarily. On many occasions in biblical writings we are told of God sending His angels to earth to deliver messages to those whom He loved. Why would it be so incredulous to believe that God would send an angel to you, in the form of your loved one, to give you that comfort that you need, that reassurance that all is well, so that you can then go on with life? If you have seen your loved one, do not be afraid. All is well. God could have sent His own angels to assure you of his or her well-being and to comfort you at this time of need. Regardless of what that experience is, you are not alone. It is a common experience and one that often is greatly comforting.

What, then, can be considered lovely about this heart-rending experience that grips your very soul with severe pain and overwhelming fear and loneliness? What can be considered lovely about having visions or hallucinations of your loved ones in the room with you? What is lovely if you dream about them as though they were much younger and much healthier? First, you must realize that if you had not loved deeply, you would not grieve your loss with such intensity. Although these two emotional experiences are diametrically opposed, they are linked together in such a way that you seldom experience true love without experiencing the pain that the loss of that loved one brings with it. Second, you must realize that there is a definite difference between intense emotion and mental illness. When you experience grief, you experience the pain of your loss in waves that tend to come and go. Much of the time you are able to function in a manner that is normal to you, completing many of your everyday tasks of living. Most people do heal in time and are able to go on with life. With mental illness, the healing is much less sure, the disorder is constantly present, and even when the illness is kept under control with medications and counseling, there is a tendency for it to return in time. So, it is lovely to know that you will recover from this loss yet not forget that one you loved so dearly. Third, having such feelings can be a key to learning how to open yourself to others or to become more dependent upon the very source of strength—God, Himself. That is a lovely position in which to find yourself.

God,

I feel as though I am losing my mind. I can't think clearly. I am confused one minute and then angry another. I don't know how to do whatever it takes to keep on living. I think that I might need to go into some sort of hospital for the mentally ill. I don't want anyone to know what a wreck I am. Everybody I see thinks I am doing so great. But, God, you know how I really am. I can't stop crying. I can't stop wishing life were different. I can't eat. I can't sleep without having nightmares. I keep seeing my spouse in my dreams, and when I wake up I think that it has been real. Will things ever be normal again? Help me, please. Give me strength to live through this hellish time. Help me to understand. Help me to see the beauty in this experience. Amen.

Fear

Fear—Friend or Foe? . . .
Consider that which is lovely!

Today may be a bleak day in which you feel fearful and uncertain. You may not know what it is that you fear, or you may try to name it. Often you fear that you may never be loved again or you fear that you will have to live with loneliness, confusion, or anger for the rest of your life. You fear that business affairs will not be completed successfully and that you will not have enough money to live out your life. You fear that you were not a good enough spouse or loved one; you fear what might happen to you if you become sick or injured. You may even fear that you will never know what to do with your life now that your loved one is dead.

Fear or apprehension can paralyze you if you allow them to, or they can motivate you to action. Consider that which is good and lovely. Would you rather be paralyzed, or would you rather take some action to help dissolve that awful monster named "*Fear*"? You may have had experiences in which you have been panic stricken, confused and almost paralyzed after reading notices from the government or hospitals or attorneys that you have not understood or have had little experience handling during marriage. The cure? Find out what you can do to take action, and then take it. You will be amazed at how quickly your fear turns from paralysis to a sense of control and calmness. You will be proud of your ability to resolve issues, which you thought you did not understand.

Perhaps you don't even know where to start the action. Wait patiently. Waiting patiently helps your mind to come to a state of peace. Think. Thinking logically of how to deal with the situations that are new and strange allows you to dissolve your fear and reach some logical conclusions. Eventually you will know what to do, and you will become empowered to do it. This is not true only with business matters, but also with matters of the heart. Do not sit idly, wringing your hands and thinking that life will never be the same. You already *know* it is not quite the same. Quit wringing and start ringing. Not everything has changed. Look around you. Do that which you used to do anyway. Oh, you may find yourself grumbling when you are doing it alone, but chances are you often have done that very same thing alone a time or two. You are quite capable; if not now, then perhaps with some experience you will become quite capable of handling life in a new and lovely way. You will make mistakes, but knowing that you have overcome the biggest obstacle—*Fear*—you will be able to move on again.

When you choose to sing the song of life, fear cannot conquer you. It may try to hold you in its embrace for a short while, but consider that which is lovely and good, and use it for your good.

> "For God has not given us a spirit of fear; but of power, and of love, and of a sound mind."
>
> -2 Timothy 1:7 (NKJV)

The Monster Called "Fear"

Fear is that monster that grabs you too tight,
Making you think you cannot do right.
But fear is just an emotion—still.
That you can overcome, if you will.
Fear would like for you to believe
There is not a thing that you can achieve.
Don't let fear conquer your soul.
You will succeed as you become whole.

Helen S. Peterson

Afraid to Go On

Consider that which is lovely!

There are times during bereavement that you feel strong and capable of handling life, but there are also those times that you may feel weak and too afraid to go on. You might be surprised on a certain day when you feel as though you are just going to crumble, and instead you stand tall and strong. Then, there comes the day when nothing unusual has occurred, but you feel as though you are just a little child, learning how to walk again. In many ways that is true. There are situations you must face that tear you apart emotionally, but they would have been so easy for your loved one. There are questions that roll around in your brain: What am I going to do with the rest of my life? Where will the pathway lead? Will I ever feel comfortable being by myself, with no one special to love me? Will I be able to handle finances so that I can take care of myself? Will I be able to cook for just one person? Will I ever be a part of a social group again? Will my life ever be normal, the way it used to be?

By focusing on questions that engender fear, you tend to rob yourself of vital energy that could and should be put into new life. This sort of fear comes from having to learn a new way of functioning, different from the old, comfortable way to which you had grown accustomed. When children are just learning to walk, they generally do not stand on their feet one day and say, "Well, today I will walk." No, instead they hold on to furniture or to their parents' hands. They stumble and they fall, but they never give up. Each time they try the new skill, they become a little more adept at it. Sometimes they scrape their knees or knock their heads. Then they hold back for a little while to recover before trying again. When they finally learn to walk alone, they don't stop there. They practice running and jumping and skipping and hopping—and, this is what you will do, too.

Indeed it is lovely that God has created us with a drive to renew ourselves and to push on in spite of difficulties. If we are His adopted children, then His Spirit lives within us to give us guidance and comfort. By focusing on Him as the Father who cares, who guides you, and who holds your hand when the walking is difficult, you practice the skills that He needs for you to learn so that you become the fulfilled human being He designed you to be. As you focus on each little step you take successfully, the joy of growth begins to emerge. With growth comes more confidence and less fear of failure. As time goes on, you find that those things you feared the most were really simple tasks that you needed to accomplish to work out the bigger

Fear

plan for your life. As you gain the confidence that comes with growth, you generally find that living life without your loved one is not so threatening. Just as hope for the future is built upon successful past experiences, so courage and strength are built upon a willingness to face those situations that make you feel weak and afraid.

Remember, all the tomorrows of your life have got to pass God before they can get to you.

> "The Lord watches over you–the Lord is your shade at your right hand . . . The Lord will keep you from all harm-he will watch over your life; the Lord will watch over your coming and going, both now and forevermore."
> -Psalm 121:5, 7-8 (NIV)

> "The truth is that our finest moments are likely to occur when we are feeling deeply uncomfortable, unhappy or unfulfilled. For it is only in such moments, propelled by our discomfort, that we are likely to step out of our ruts and start searching for different ways or truer answers."
> -M. Scott Peck. *90.*

When Fear of the Future Robs Your Joy . . .
Consider that which is lovely!

You, like most of us, probably do not enjoy radical change in your relationships, so when you find yourself facing the future alone, you often focus on the uncertainties of tomorrow, which then causes you to live your life filled with fear and anxiety. You may rush to relieve such fear by becoming dangerously occupied with activities that take up your time, but which do not enrich your soul and spirit. Some people rush to avoid the fear which change has created by almost immediately jumping into a new relationship that is not always the best or the wisest.

Adolph was a man who had been married for over sixty years. He had lovingly cared for his dear wife for almost ten years as her health declined, and she became more and more incapacitated. Shortly after her death, he met a woman thirty years his junior. Seeking to fill that great fear of living alone created by the absence of his beloved spouse, he coaxed the woman into marrying him just three months after the death of his first wife. Three months of married life went by, and one day he arrived back in the house after completing some errands to find that his new wife had left, vowing never to come back. He tried and tried to get her to come back to him, to no avail. Now he continues to live with the pain of several losses as well as with a fear of living life alone. What went wrong?

Unfortunately, the dear man had tried to eliminate the fear of loneliness by filling his life with someone else. He had chosen unwisely, thinking that a younger woman might also care for him as he had cared for his late wife. Searching frantically for relief from the fear of living life alone, he had abandoned reason and wise thinking for immediate release from the pain.

Grieving is not fun. Grieving is hard work. It consumes your energy and relentlessly tears at your heart. The emptiness of life alone can cause great fear often described as pain. But, to run from the pain can often precipitate even greater pain in the long run. While God never intended for you to grieve, He did know it would happen and He did build into you a means of healing if you are just patient enough to allow that healing to take place.

The beauty of living through your grief is that while you become more dependent upon God for relief from the pain, you also become more resourceful, using your individual talents and abilities to help yourself to grow. At the same time as you become more dependent upon God, you also develop more confidence and self-reliance, which results in more independence. Out of your weakness, you develop new strengths. Out of your fears, you develop more courage. Out of your loneliness, you develop more resourcefulness to fill those times of loneliness with activities and relationships that nourish your spirit. Out of your willingness to change, you develop flexibility that enables you to face life with more zest and more zeal than you have ever known before.

When you fear the future, embrace the joy of today. Consider that which is lovely around you. Wait patiently for healing to take place. Move ahead with resolution to grow and to face your new life with great courage.

When you have no hope for the future, You have no power in the present. Hope is based upon remembering those good things that you have seen happen in the past. They provide light for the future.

Facing Life Alone

I was afraid that I could not face the future without you–yet here I am.
I was afraid the guilt and pain would not end—but they have.
I was afraid I would not stop dreaming about you at night–and I have.
I never thought I would have energy to live normally again–but I do.
I never thought I could pay the bills and deal with business matters–yet I have learned how to do that.
I never thought I could sell a house or a car or anything without you—yet I have made several sales.
I never thought that I would travel alone to far off places without you—yet I have traveled to Egypt and to Europe alone.
I never believed I would be a part of a group of friends again–but I am.
I never believed that I would be able to laugh at silly things–but I have.
I never believed I would develop any new talents after you died–yet I am doing that.
I always wondered if life would be lonely—it has been.
I always wondered if I could overcome the loneliness—most of the time, yes.
I always wondered if my life would hold any new challenges–it has.
I always wondered if I could be successful without you–I have been.
I miss you. I think of you. I take joy in the fact that your healing is complete.
I remember the skills you demonstrated and find they are an important part of me.
I am glad!
I will always love you.
I am not afraid anymore.
I face the future joyfully.
I will see you in eternity.

Helen S. Peterson

Wondering If Your Spouse Would Approve . . .
Consider that which is lovely!

After living with your spouse for years, whether it is two or fifty-two, when you love that person dearly, you generally want to do that which is acceptable to the other. Even though the other has died, often you go on measuring your life by whether he or she would approve of that which you are doing. Living this way often limits you from making decisions that you would like to or need to make. At times, that may be a good thing. But, more often than not, your own decision about a matter is just as good, though perhaps not as practical or aesthetic or cost effective as the other person's might have been. But now, without the security of acceptance from the other, you are a bit tottery. Sometimes you are totally indecisive because you have relied too much on the approval of the other. You must learn to think through that which is good and wise from your past. Using good learning is respectful and appropriate. Yet, now is the time to go on alone. Now is the time to give *yourself* the approval that you need because of *your* good thinking. You are the one who continues to live in this world, and therefore you must approve of the decisions that you make.

How can you overcome the habit that you have formed of trying to please the other because you loved him or her? How can you relinquish your need for approval? How rid yourself of the guilt you feel when you do what *you* want to do instead of what your spouse would have wanted you to do? What is lovely at all about this dilemma in which you now find yourself?

The lovely part is that you have learned much as you lived your life with your spouse or your loved one. You have gained great insight and knowledge into many areas of life. If it were not true, you wouldn't be questioning yourself at this time. When we are able to question our decisions, we are then thinking of what would be best for us at the time based upon the knowledge that we have. When your spouse was alive, there were two persons to consider. Now there is only you. When your spouse was alive, you might have done things to make the other happy; now you must do that which makes you feel content and satisfied within. You must do that which is right without getting the approval of your spouse. You are fully capable of moving ahead with confidence because you have stopped to think through your decisions. You have decided that they are good for you at this time in your life.

This is a time of testing yourself and your own ability to think well. It is also a time to look to God's word, the Bible, to be sure that your decision is not against

His perfect will. It may be a time to consult with dear friends whom you have come to trust as you have progressed through this period in your life. But, remember, ultimately it is a time to take a leap of faith and do those things that you might not have tried to do before.

> "Forgetting what is behind, and straining toward what is ahead, I press on toward the goal to win the prize for which God has called me heavenward in Christ Jesus."
>
> -Philippians 3:13–14 (NIV)

Hearing God Speak

Life is so confusing;
It causes us to frown.
The world around us clamors;
The noise just gets us down.

We seek for the right pathway,
Amidst the "free for all."
We're faced with many choices,
Some of which could cause a fall.

There is a wondrous secret
To knowing how to choose
Between the "wrong" that pulls us
And the "right" that we might lose.

You must *listen to the voice*
That speaks from deep within,
And check what it is saying
To be sure it is not sin.

You must *choose a trusted few*
To add wisdom to the voice.
It will become so clear
When you want to do God's choice.

You must *watch for signs without*
That will show you God's own way,
And when you see these three,
You must be on your knees to pray.

God will give you peace
If His will you want to do.
My friend, you *can* expect it,
When to His Word you're true.

Helen S. Peterson

ANGER

Why Did God Take *My* Loved One? . . .
Consider that which is lovely!

When you experience the pain of your loss, sometimes you question, however briefly, why God chose to take *your* loved one instead of someone else. Although you know that God is sovereign and that He has a purpose in all He allows to happen to you, you still feel angry and forsaken. You cannot assuage the pain from your loss simply by saying, "It was for the better. It was God's will." You must gain some new truth from your questioning so that you are able to live through the pain and grow as a result of it.

Dr. Henry Blackaby has noted in his book *Created to be God's Friend* that "Sometimes God has to 'remove' others from your lives, so He can continue His purposes for your lives" (p. 48). He used the life of Abraham as an example to illustrate his statement. Abraham's father died while they were traveling toward the land that was promised to Abraham and to the nation of Israel. No doubt, Abraham really wanted his father along on this journey of faith that he had begun. We do not know much about Terah, but from the character that Abraham had developed, you might assume that Terah had been a good Godly father. You might assume that he had taught his son well about how to survive life in the desert. You could believe that he had a relationship with Abraham that was deep and respectful. No doubt Abraham hoped that his father also would have been able to enter that Promised Land that God had sent him to obtain. Probably Abraham was hurt that God had taken that privilege away from his dad. Perhaps Abraham also got a little angry with God because He had promised to "multiply his seed as the stars above," and now his future children would be deprived of ever seeing or knowing their granddad. No doubt Abraham also questioned God as to why he would have let his father "tear up his roots" and come all the way from home to Haran, just to let him die in a strange place. No doubt Abraham grieved deeply that his father was no longer with him—perhaps to give him good advice about life in the desert, perhaps just for good companionship, perhaps just so that he could help bear the burdens of moving his entire family and belongings to a strange and distant place.

Abraham may have asked some of the same questions that you and I would ask. Why would a kind and loving God allow such things to happen to His children? Could not He, with all of His power and wisdom, get His purpose fulfilled without you having to go through deep grief? Why would He, who is supposed to be merciful, sometimes take several loved ones within a short time span? Doesn't He realize there is a limit to how much grief an individual can bear at any given time? Why would God deprive your loved ones of seeing the promise of life fulfilled in their children and in their children's children?

Because Abraham no longer had the responsibility of a relationship with his father, he was spurred on to leave Haran, where perhaps he had become somewhat comfortable, and to travel south toward his final destination. Sometimes, God allows you to "lose" your loved ones, those upon whom you depend, in order to help you to clarify your values in life or in order for you to become more dependent upon Him for love. Sometimes He removes loved ones in order for you to have to reach out to others whom you may never have considered to be capable of providing love or support. Sometimes He takes away loved ones in order for you to examine your own attitudes and to make changes within. There are times when he removes those upon whom you depend in order to shake you from your inertia and to move you ahead, unencumbered and with more intensity, to fulfill His purposes for your life.

What could be more beautiful and lovely than knowing that God cares so much about you that He is willing to allow adversity to enter into your life in order to perfect you? As a child of God, you can trust that He is in control and you will never experience more adversity than He needs to allow in order to mold you into a beautiful "diamond" for Him. You are His treasured jewel, and even though you may feel deserted, you know that:

> "[God] has said, 'I will never leave you and I will never abandon you.'
> So we can say with confidence, 'The Lord is my helper, and I will not be afraid. What can man do to me?'"
>
> -Hebrews 13:5–6 (NET)

Moving Toward the Crown

> Will the battles of life ever be oe'r?
> Not till the war is won.
> Will the struggles continue forever more?
> Yes, till the setting sun.
>
> Will my pain and loneliness ever cease?
> Yes, in time you will heal.

Will I, with loved ones, again feel at peace?
Love is the mending seal.

Will there ever be life in life again?
Yes, in various ways.
Will I ever see sunshine without the rain?
Sunlight follows gloomy days.

Will life hold happiness, joy and peace?
Yes, when the Master is known.
Will I make it through this long dark place?
Yes. As you keep moving toward the Crown.

Helen S. Peterson

Questioning the Love of Your Spouse . . .
Consider that which is lovely!

    In ninety-nine percent of marriages there are times of disagreement, some arguments, and even periods of discord. This is normal as we work to blend different personalities and backgrounds while attempting to rear families, secure possessions, and fulfill successful careers. During your times of grieving however, sometimes doubts may arise as to whether or not your spouse really loved you or if he or she merely stayed with you through the years in order to fulfill obligations to the children, expectations of others, or to remain in a comfort zone because it would have been even harder to change. Such thoughts may come when you are tired, when you feel lonely, or maybe even when you have a moment of feeling sorry for yourself and your loss. They are thoughts that are linked to unrealistic feelings of guilt for not having been a perfect spouse at all times. They are thoughts that are linked to feelings of doubt about yourself and your value now that you are widowed. They are negative thoughts that often occur when your chemical balances are not in proper working order because of the stress of grief, and they are thoughts that catch you off guard in a most overwhelming manner.
    Can there really be something lovely gained from having such thoughts and feelings? Yes. On these occasions, it is extremely valuable to remember all the good times that you spent with your spouse. It is valuable to remember that when you married, you both pledged to live with and love each other "for better or for worse." It is helpful to remember that your spouse also was not perfect, although you might choose to think he or she was at this point in time. It is important to realize that love is not always a feeling, but as with God's love toward us, it is a commitment. There are times when you chose to love your spouse or your children in spite of how they behaved toward you. And so it was with your spouse toward you.
    It is a relief when you realize that you did not need to be perfect in order to have been loved. It is also wonderful to be able to learn from the mistakes of the past and to resolve not to make those same errors in the future. Of course, you must realize, that even if you don't make those same errors, you will make other errors! That happens because we are all human. Most of all, it is important to remember that together you did your best to weather the storms of marriage. That is the test of true love.
    A good thing to do to help bring back the good memories, even if your marriage was broken in some ways, is to look through photos of happy times. Talk with

others about fun experiences you had, and then choose to believe that love was real. Also, understand that chronic illness and emotional issues may make a person less pleasant and less able to express love toward anyone. Take joy in the remembrance of all that is good in the past, and rejoice in the hope of new life and new challenges in the present and the future.

The Answer to Questions about Your Love

Thank you, Father, for the love you have given
For the new understanding, so clear and so deep.
Thank you, Jesus. I love you,
For I know it's a promise You'll keep.

Prepare me now for life's fullness
So the depth of your love I will know.
Open my life and remake me,
Teach me, in patience, to grow.

Father, your love is too great for me.
I cannot understand.
And yet you've promised it all
If I'll just keep hold of your hand.

And so I will, dear Father.
No matter how long it may be.
I love you so, my Father.
I believe your promise I'll see.

Helen S. Peterson

When Acceptance Won't Come . . .
Consider that which is lovely!

Today I am sad and angry. I woke up thinking that my spouse was there lying next to me and looked over to see an empty place where once he lay. He has been gone for eleven years now. Yet, at times I have difficulty accepting the idea. My brain tells me that he is dead. I know he died on Christmas Day. I know we buried him on his birthday. I know he has not been here to help me pay the bills or to make decisions during these past years. I have not shared his presence here beside me. He has not enjoyed the things that I have done since he left this earth. I know he is dead, but my heart doesn't want to accept his absence. I still want him to be with me. I miss him. I feel so badly that I did not fully appreciate him and all of his talents before he died—while he was still alive for me to tell him how much I admired him.

Perhaps you have gone through times such as these. Have you found it difficult to believe that your loved one is gone permanently? Why is that? Perhaps you don't want to face that reality because it makes you keenly aware of our own mortality. Perhaps you still have unresolved emotional issues with which you must deal before you can let go of feelings such as anger, guilt, or resentment. Perhaps you think that there must be some way to make up for what you did not do or how you did not act during the time of your marriage. Maybe you feel that by holding on to your grief, you can punish yourself for not having been as good a wife or husband as you might have been. Maybe you even believe that if you don't feel the pain that means that you didn't love enough. Maybe if you accept the permanency of the loss it means that you are forgetting about that loved one. There are a myriad of reasons why you sometimes have difficulty letting go of a deceased loved one. Many are based on your false assumptions of how life is supposed to be.

Questioning is a part of the bereavement process. It is normal and necessary. So, let us look at what is lovely about this questioning process. As you reflect upon your loss and your inability to accept that loss, you can realize how precious life really is. You can gain a new appreciation for those who are still alive and a part of your life. It is wonderful, if because of your lack of acceptance, you vow to make more of each remaining day. If you can learn to make better choices in your life:of your friends, of your words, and of your actions, knowing that they really do make a difference when all is said and done, then that is a lovely result of the learning that is taking place. The good and wonderful part of this painful process is that it can be a time of new growth, a time of new awakening to the wonders of life and love. A vital part of that growth can be new ways of thinking about life and new, more realistic expectations for yourself and others.

While you may feel as though you are drowning in sorrow, the will to survive works within you causing you to move ahead, however slowly. The lack of acceptance gives you time to grow emotionally in spite of the fact that you are still struggling with the loss. Hope does continue to burn in your heart even though the flame may be tiny. Such hope is not unfounded. You will survive. You will wake up one morning less sad, less regretful, and feeling more alive, alert, and ready to begin life again as you make a realistic assessment of the causes for prolonging your grief. You will know that your loved one is gone from this earth, but that as long as you are still here, you have a purpose or a mission to fulfill. You will know that even though you cannot express your love and appreciation, you still have your memories of good times and good experiences.

Questions That Have No Answers

Quite often in the course of life the way seems so unclear.
Questions have no answers, which causes us to fear.
We staunchly fight with dignity to soothe away the pain,
But then we find to no avail it plaques us all the same.

Though we count on faith in God, and strength from those so dear,
Something within us trembles still when solutions are not clear.
Outwardly we smile and say the words so right,
But no one knows that deep within there wars a lonely fight.

We've learned to mask our feelings and don a phony grin,
The saying goes, "Old Fellow, take it on the chin!"
Oh, if they could only see the pain we bear alone,
There'd be more understanding if they too revealed their own.

Quite often in the course of life the answers do not please
It's then we beg and plead with God, our desires to appease.
We bargain and get angry, and sometimes even cry...
Questioning the course of life, demanding to know "why?"

The times within the course of life when answers satisfy,
Complacently we go our way and never question "why?"
It seems we do not understand, when life is fraught with pain,
Those are the richest times for us, the times of greatest gain.

Most often in the course of life the answers take some time,
If we would share our doubts and fears, together we would climb.
The way through painful times would ease, the joys would multiply,
Our journey through the course of life we could simplify.

Helen S. Peterson

When You Are Very Angry . . .
Consider that which is lovely!

Have you ever been so angry that you wanted to punch anyone within your reach? Hopefully there was no one there to punch, so you could not. I imagine that it was lucky for them and lucky for you.

Feeling anger is a natural part of grief. We become angry when we are suddenly pushed out of our comfort zone and have to struggle to learn how to live life in a new and different manner. We become angry when we have to shoulder all the responsibility for life's business without the comforting presence of our companion. We become angry that we no longer have that person whom we loved, and we never will again. We become angry when we think that others are just going on with their lives and may be taking advantage of our kindness and vulnerability. We become angry when those whom we have helped in the past don't seem to be there in the present to help *us*. We become angry when we feel helpless and out of control, and we think we are not able to do anything to change the situation. We become angry when others seem to demand our time, and we are too tired from this grief "stuff" even to help ourselves.

How can you turn all those feelings of anger into what is lovely? Understanding the sources of your anger is your first step. Generally the root of this type of anger is fear. You are afraid that you are not going to be able to function alone, without the help or love of that person whom you loved. You are afraid that you are going to feel the deep pain of this loss for the rest of your life. You are afraid that no one will ever love you again as he or she did. You are afraid that they have already forgotten that you ever existed—wherever they are. You worry about where they are and whether God really answered your prayers for them. Because you feel alone and lost, you think no one else can ever understand the pain you are experiencing. And that, too, makes you angry. Often your anger becomes generalized until once again you regain emotional balance. Other people don't like the angry you, and you surely don't like yourself.

Once you realize that most of your fears are lies that you tell yourself, then you can begin to turn the anger into something lovely. You can take small actions to prove to yourself that you can handle the responsibilities, however long it may take you to learn. You can look at others who have come through their losses and realize that somehow they are joyful again, and so you, too, can seek for ways to experience that joy again. You can remember those who have once again found love and purpose in their lives, and from them, take hope that one day you will find the same. You can remember the wonderful love that you still cherish from years of experiences together. You can remind yourself that someday in heaven you will be reunited, and you will recognize each other and rejoice to see each other. The scripture also tells you that there will be no tears in heaven. That doesn't help the present, but it does give you hope for the future.

Just as there is balance in all of nature, you can look forward to that day when once again you will find that balance in a new way of life for yourself. There may never be another spouse, definitely not like the one you lost, but God promises to supply your need and to calm your fears in this regard.

It is okay to be angry for a short time. It is not okay to use that anger to hurt others or to hurt yourself. It is wise to realize that life is continually changing and when you change with it, you will find yourself less angry and more peaceful.

> "Praise be to the God and Father of our Lord Jesus Christ, the Father of compassion and the God of all comfort, who comforts us in all our troubles, so that we can comfort those in any trouble with the comfort we ourselves have received from God. For just as the sufferings of Christ flow over into our lives, so also through Christ our comfort overflows."
>
> -2 Corinthians 1:3–5 (NIV)

Wondering Where You Are

> As I gaze toward the heavens at the first evening star,
> I longingly wonder if that's where you are.
> I can't imagine where heaven might be,
> But wherever you are, it is peaceful and free.
> I know you're with God and our Savior dear,
> So those special thoughts never are drear.
>
> But, each time I return from my chores 'round the town
> I want to call out, "Hi Love. I'm home."
> Sometimes I do . . . no one answers my call.
> So I walk through the house, down the long empty hall.

I miss you so much when I lie down to sleep
Can't hear you snoring, not even a peep.
I miss you when unfamiliar turf I have trod,
And then I remember that you're there with God.

Sometimes I wish you were back here to stay,
But now you've seen a glorious new Way.
For you to come back would cause you such pain
As you saw through new eyes the sin and the shame.
That's why when I gaze toward the first evening star,
I sing praises to God that you are where you are.

Helen S. Peterson

Angry with God . . .
                              Consider that which is lovely!

You may be feeling so angry right now that you would like to kick over the flowerpot or even worse, kick the dog. So what are you really angry about? I found myself feeling furious one weekend evening when I had spent the entire day alone and generally felt as though I had accomplished nothing. I was lonely and lacking motivation to do all the things that I thought were important to do. I was frustrated because I even had to do them. Oh, I was so angry with God for having taken my loved one away from me that I shouted at the top of my lungs and asked Him why He had left me alone and forsaken. I told Him that He could have healed him and not have left me in this lonely condition. He could have taken someone else, not my loved one.

Once the energy from my angry self-pity had dissipated, I was able to turn the situation around and tell God how much I thanked Him for relieving my loved one from the difficult aspects of life. I was able to tell Him that I really hated the loneliness, but that if that was His plan for right now, I would accept it because He knows what is best to help me to grow and to become more in touch with Him. I thanked Him for the life that I have and for the ability to talk or to listen or to think. I thanked Him for allowing me to feel anger because then I knew I was fully alive and functioning.

Finally, I ended up chuckling about my anger because it motivated me to start cleaning the mess I had made in the house during my lonely days. It motivated me to water the plants that I had long neglected because of my temporary withdrawal from life. It motivated me to get into bed earlier than usual to get a good long night's sleep. And it motivated me to start a regular regime of exercise each day so that I might be able to relieve some of the tension of loneliness and hurt that had generated the anger. What a wonderful blessing it turned out to be.

Consider that which is lovely. You may experience some of my kind of anger. You do not have to remain angry just because you think that God has treated you wrongly. You do not have to join the ranks of inertia just because you don't like what has happened. God is big enough to understand your frustration and resulting fury. He will help you to help you turn your anger into a gold mine that will make you richer forever. Go ahead and shout at Him. Cry out to Him in your anger. Let Him know how you feel. He is willing to listen to you. All He wants for you is the best life. He knows what that life entails, even when sadness and loss are a part of it.

When your anger is all released, then turn your anger into good things and go on with life. That is what God wants and that is probably what your spouse would prefer for you to do.

"Be angry and sin not; Let not the sun go down upon your wrath: Neither give place to the devil."

-Ephesians 4:26–27 (NIV)

"When you pass through the waters, I will be with you; and when you pass through the rivers they will not sweep over you. When you walk through the fire, you will not be burned; the flames will not set you ablaze. For I am the Lord, your God, the Holy One of Israel, your Savior."

-Isaiah 43:2 (NIV)

Strength Follows Weakness!

We've learned that weakness is really bad;
We must hide our feelings when we are sad.
We must hide our grief from the world to see
While inside we are dying silently.

The world would prefer that we stuff and deny.
The world would prefer that we never would cry.
But there is a limit to how much pain we can bear
Without breaking down and needing to share.

But finding someone with empathic heart
Is really a chore that we dare not start.
So we turn to addictions, like liquor or food
To ease our pain and change our mood.

For a little while we don't feel the great ache,
But again the pain comes while asleep or awake.
We learn that our methods will not help us heal
They just numb our senses so we cannot feel.

It is in our weakness that we become strong
When we turn to God who is there all along.
We ask for healing from the terrible pain.
From out of our weakness great strength we gain!

We learn at last what strong people can feel—
That in our weakness we can be healed.
Our strength will emerge from deep inside
From our great weakness we need never hide!

Helen S. Peterson

When Your Sorrow Makes You Bitter . . .
Consider that which is lovely!

In the course of your grieving you may have had some very negative thoughts and behaviors. You may have become angry and alienated from friends and family members who have disappointed you. You may have questioned God's plan for your life. You may have challenged God as to why He has taken your spouse from you. By allowing yourself to think negatively, you may have become a bitter person. Bitterness is generally the result of incorrect thinking.

Have you ever thought that maybe God didn't design marriage or human relationships to make us *happy*, but instead, to make us *holy*? Of course, it wasn't a part of His original plan. When he originally put us on this earth we were holy. Originally, He planned to have us live in Paradise where we didn't have to work so hard to have the good things. But, unfortunately that was ruined, and a backup plan was put into place. Have you ever thought that perhaps sorrow is a part of the plan to draw us back to Him and to the state that He had originally planned for humans? Have you ever thought that perhaps you relied too heavily on the love of a human and not enough on the love of God? Is there a chance that you just did not really understand compassion or the sorrow of others until you experienced your great loss?

God is a holy God, and He desires that we become more like Him each day. He knows that we are a stubborn group, and that we cherish our independence so we can prove how capable we really are. But, there comes a time when He wants you to realize that you can depend upon His promises to help you survive your time on this earth. He wants you to be more desirous of being totally committed to your mission and more desirous of serving Him wholeheartedly. He wants you to be happy, but more than that, He wants you to be holy. Holiness is the ultimate state of happiness because in that condition you can have wonderful communion with Him.

It is true that when you have particular humans in your life to love, you tend to focus on what makes them and you happy. Your energies are limited, so in focusing on earthly things you dilute the focus on heavenly things. When your loved one was here on this earth, perhaps you spent a lot of time devoted to your spouse and just a fraction of your time devoted to God. It is wonderful to know that now you are able to spend more time turning to God so that He can teach you how to cope with your loss. It is lovely that now you have more time to appreciate the gifts that He gave to you through the life of your loved one as well as within your own self. At this sad time in your life, perhaps you may learn the real secret of happiness. Perhaps by growing in your love of God and your knowledge of whose you really are, you will be able to gain even more riches while you continue to live out your mission on earth. Perhaps the loveliest thing to think about is that one day you will be reunited with those whom you have loved on this earth. They will have the joy of knowing a much more mature, more God-like person than that whom they left behind when they departed from this earth.

Do not be discouraged. God has great and wonderful plans for your life. Sorrow may be just another way that He uses to bring those wonderful plans to fruition. Allow yourself to grieve appropriately and then, when the time comes, continue to grow and to prepare yourself for a fruitful and satisfying life to come. Remember that when you are filled with God's love there is no room for you to be bitter.

> Bitterness imprisons life; love releases it. Bitterness paralyzes life; love empowers it. Bitterness sours life; love sweetens it. Bitterness sickens life; love heals it. Bitterness blinds life; love anoints its eyes.
>
> Harry Emerson Fosdick.

The Loving Way

Many voices crying, many hearts are dying.
Many deeds are breaking lives in two.
But, crying hearts are mended and broken lives are healed
When God's great love is channeled through folks like me and you.

Loving is not something that humans do so well.
If we counted on *our* loving, we'd all be doomed to hell.
Loving comes through knowing the One who gave His life
To cleanse us from our sinful selves and heal our deeds of strife.

Loving means commitment when feelings fade away.
Loving means we "stay the course" when we'd rather go astray.
Loving means we hold on to all that's good and right
And show the kindness others need in darkness of the night.

Loving means when all is said and done,
We give our love to others as God willingly gave His son.
God can see the motives, God can see the heart.
It's not for us to be the judge, but to simply do our part.

Helen S. Peterson

GUILT

When You Feel Guilty because You Feel Relieved . . .
Consider that which is lovely!

If you have been the caretaker of your loved one who has died, it is quite likely you will feel a sense of relief soon after he or she has died. When caring for that person over a long period of time, no doubt you have given up some of the normal activities that had been a part of your life or of both of your lives. You are undoubtedly extremely tired and need change in your life activities. The sudden release from that responsibility is so welcome. Yet, once you obtain that freedom, you may feel lost or confused, and dreadfully guilty because you *feel* so relieved to be free. It is almost as if you are saying to your loved one, "You were such a burden." It may have been true at times, but overall, you probably do not feel that way. Feeling relieved is actually a very healthy feeling because it is facing the reality that the dying process was not only hard on the one who died, but it was also hard on you.

However, because you tell yourself you should feel sad, it is then that your mind can start playing tricks with you. Those who have lived with a dying person have generally experienced anticipatory grief. That means that you have been grieving all the while that your loved one has been ill and moving toward death. Therefore, the reaction of sadness is not always present when the loved one dies. Beware, guilt is a great deceiver. Your undeserved feelings of guilt rob you of the conviction that you needed to do a job and that you did it well. You may tell yourself you should have or could have done more to help. You may have great remorse because at times you got downright angry or even mildly irritated with the person or with the situation. You may wish you had called in other medical experts to assess your loved one's condition with the possibility that he or she could have lived longer had you done something differently. There is no end to the lies that can come into your mind.

First, do not regard yourself as unusual. Just about everyone who cares finds something they might have done better. Second, do not allow yourself to *dwell* on what you could have, should have done, or might have done. Think on the lovely side. You did what you could, with the resources that you had, to make that loved one feel comfortable and loved. Yes, you may have gotten irritated or short with words at times, but overall, you showed love and care. That person benefited from having you there by them as they were declining in health. You may have been the only one to provide nourishment or to bathe them or help them get out of bed and to get dressed. You may have been the only one to listen to their strange ramblings. You may have resented that you had to carry the burden yourself when others could have helped had they chosen to do so. Don't chide yourself for this feeling. It was hard work, and you probably did need more help. But, your loved one needed *you,* and you were there, perhaps not every minute, but as much as you could be. Yours was the hand they held or the voice to which they responded. They felt your presence even when they could not speak or move. They knew you loved them and you were there with them as they made the transition from this world into the next.

What is lovely is that you are able to choose to put the guilt away and to think of the wonderful things that you did. Think of the kind words, the good care, and the laughter you once had together. Think of the patience that you learned and of the empathy you now have for others as a result of this experience. Of course you will be sad. Of course you will grieve. But, you do not need to add guilt to that experience. Be glad that you were hand-picked by God to be the one to minister to this dear child of His. That is what makes this experience a lovely one. Others might have done the job, but they didn't. You did. You gave of yourself, mostly unselfishly, and now it is okay to feel relief.

Memo from God

To My dear Child:

I know that you have spent a great deal of time caring for your loved one who is now in heaven with me. I want you to go on with a healthy life, and therefore these are my instructions to you:

1. Do not fret that you did not care enough or properly. You were not in control of death. It is my decision as to when someone's mission has been completed on earth.

2. Accept any of the feelings you may now be experiencing. I did not intend for you to grieve, but I did provide you with the emotions to do so and to become healthy again. Each of your emotions serves a purpose for making you whole again.

3. Remember that I did not take you from the earth at this time because you still have much work to do for me. This training will be a part of the mission I

have for you for the future. Get back into good physical and emotional health and join the team again.

4. Know that one day I will call you to heaven and you will be reunited with all those whom you love. That is my promise to you. Be prepared.

God

When Guilt Won't Set You Free . . .
Consider that which is lovely!

There are times when guilt becomes your worst enemy. You begin to feel guilty for things you said or did that hurt your loved one. You ruminate, trying to relieve the pain that you feel because you can no longer correct that behavior. At the moment all you can remember is that you hurt him or her. You cannot even remember the forgiveness that you received.

Then there are the times when you feel severe guilt over things that you did *not* do that you might have or should have done. These thoughts just keep whirring away, filling your heart with pain. You may say to yourself, "If only I had done what he or she had wanted." You live with regret, wishing you could go back in time and make things different.

These types of thoughts are common to all who grieve. Even though you know rationally that you cannot undo the past or correct your sins of omission or commission, you still beat yourself until you feel the pain.

There are some truly good things to gain from these experiences of feeling guilt. Because you are still alive, you do have the opportunity to learn from your past mistakes. It is true that you cannot correct them in your loved one's life, but you can be aware not to make the same mistakes with others whom you love. You can become much more sensitive to those character traits within yourself that may have caused you either to do or not to do some of things in the past. Further, you can seek to be an active rather than a passive participant in life, working diligently to help yourself and others enjoy and appreciate your little "quirks" more. You can take this opportunity to make logical assessments of those situations for which you feel guilt to determine if, indeed, your guilt is valid or if it is something that you do to yourself unnecessarily. Finally, you can learn to forgive yourself for your weaknesses and shortcomings. You can seek to improve yourself so that you will live a better life while you are fulfilling your mission here on this earth.

Consider that which is lovely. By becoming more aware of yourself and how you may have lived life in the past, you have another chance to change some of those things that you regret. By recognizing how you may punish yourself when punishment is not appropriate, you can improve your relationships in the here and now, and you can appreciate that you have yet another opportunity to enrich the world around you with kindness and care in ways that you had not thought of before.

Lord,

Make us aware of how we sometimes change the facts to fit our feelings. Help us to face life with a renewed sense of who we are. As the oft-spoken phrase has put it: "There is no going back, and we can't change the past or turn back the hands of time. Yesterday is history, tomorrow is a mystery and I know that only this moment is mine." Amen.

A New Day Is Here

My world has been washed clean with the nighttime rain.
All the robins are looking for the treasures of earth,
The sunshine is beaming brightly again
As if to say to all nature "Just look at your worth."
In the peaceful hush of the morning light, my life feels fresh and new.
Indeed it is, to my delight, another chance to live and love.
Where will my pathways lead me this day?
Will my good deeds be many or few?
Opportunity may knock but once this day, and then may disappear,
I pledge me to watch most diligently for that needy one
Who will blossom and grow and move courageously from fear
As I respond most lovingly to the deed that should be done.
When the hours have past and the moments have slipped away,
I'll remember with joy that I've used well, my chance to live and love today.

Helen S. Peterson

Could Haves and Should Haves . . .
Consider that which is lovely!

When a loved one has been sick or gradually diminishing in health, you generally have done what you could to help. After they die, sometimes you think this was not enough and if you had done one more thing, it would have made the difference between life and death. Most frequently that is not true. But, what about when your loved one has been the victim of an accident? So many times you second-guess yourself saying, "If I had only done this or if I had only done that." Well, you didn't. Whether it would have made a difference or not, you do not know. Chances are that the accident that took him or her would have occurred anyway.

You often forget that you are not in control of the actions of others, no matter how much you love them or how much you think you should take care of them. You must remember that they, too, have their own minds and their own wills. They determine their own behaviors, and they live or die with the consequences of their choices.

When you say that you should have done something differently, you are actually saying that you miss their presence so much or that you wish the accident had not happened. You are saying you do not want to deal with the pain of your loss. Sometimes you are saying you wish you had said or done some things differently when you still had them alive.

Death often comes when you least expect it and for reasons that you don't understand. The important thing to learn from an unexpected death is to live each day as though it were your last. Use each opportunity to be kind and encouraging. Do today what is worthwhile and positive. As Dr. Richard Carlson has said, "Don't sweat the small stuff." Make deliberate choices to accept your loved ones just as they are with all of their faults, weaknesses, and strengths. Look beyond the bad to the good things that you know about them.

You cannot do anything about the "should haves" or "could haves." There is no sense focusing on what you might have done because either you can't change it or it would not have affected the eventual outcome, anyway. Rather you can turn your regret into a blessing. You can learn from your mistakes or perceived mistakes and become more caring in the relationships you still have or that you will continue to make as time goes by. You can forgive yourself just as God forgives you when you ask Him to. You can purpose in your heart to be more aware of the fragility of life and of the importance of the moment in which you live. By doing so, you can choose to make each moment today a rich, peaceful, and fulfilling one so that when you look back tomorrow, the memory will be sweet and satisfying. When your life has fallen to pieces, hold on to that peace which comes from above.

Only This Moment Is Mine

There's so many things we'd change if we lived our lives again,
So many things we would and would not do.
All the past mistakes we've made and the price that we have paid.
Oh, how we would live if we could start anew.

CHORUS: But there is no going back and we can't change the past,
Or turn back the hands of time.
Yesterday is history; tomorrow is a mystery,
And I know that only this moment is mine.

There are things we would never try and tears we'd never cry,
If we had known the hill was far too steep.
We'd have never tumbled down or fallen in and drowned,
If we had known the river was so deep.

But there is no going back and we can't change the past,
Or turn back the hands of time.
Yesterday is history; tomorrow is a mystery,
And I know that only this moment is mine.

So it's best if we forget the things we now regret,
For we cannot go back and change the past.
Let us use those old mistakes, a better life to make,
And tomorrow we may find that dream at last.

For there is no going back and we can't change the past,
Or turn back the hands of time.
Yesterday is history; tomorrow is a mystery,
And I know that only this moment is mine.

Daniel O'Donell. Lyrics and music *Only This Moment is Mine*

When You Have Made a Major Mistake . . .
Consider that which is lovely!

Sometimes, when experiencing the pain of your loss, you make decisions that are not really the wisest ones to make. You often make those decisions to help you to deal with your pain, or you make those decisions to try to launch out on your own. Both reasons are acceptable and admirable. Sometimes those decisions or choices are very beneficial although they may be hard to deal with. However, at other times, your decisions may lead you into more pain because you are not yet ready to experience the consequences. Perhaps it is at those times that you have not really thought through what your decisions might entail.

Just now you may be experiencing the pain of a decision you have made. It may seem that your world has turned upside down—again. Perhaps your decision has cost you a great deal of money or great embarrassment or chagrin. Perhaps your decision has begun to take you down a wrong path in life. You may be feeling worthless or foolish or incapable of living your life well. Do not worry. Instead, turn your experience into a gold mine.

Yes, even when you make poor decisions, you can gain from them. Consider the learning that has come from the situation. Consider that you were courageous enough to move on with life, even if the moving was not quite the right path to take at the time. Give yourself great commendation for having had that courage. You did not sit back and vegetate. You did not go into hibernation.

Consider the fact that your decision was a step forward in life and not backward. Consider that now you have a new perspective of some facet of life that you did not have previously. Consider that not all of the consequences of your decision were negative. Perhaps you met new people, had a new adventure, or perhaps learned how to better manage your finances. Perhaps your decision has caused you to take a little more care in making future decisions. Perhaps you have learned to be more communicative with someone because of your pain. These are the lovely consequences of making mistakes in life.

All is not lost, and much has been gained. Everyone, regardless of whether they are grieving or not, makes mistakes. Not everyone learns from them. Rejoice that you are one who does learn. Yesterday is past, never to be lived again. Tomorrow is not yet here. Today is what you have. Be at peace and live with zest in this moment of time.

Whenever you make a mistake or get knocked down by life, don't look back at it too long. Mistakes are life's way of teaching you. Your capacity for occasional blunders is inseparable from your capacity to reach your goals. No one wins them all, and your failures, when they happen, are just part of your growth. Shake off your blunders. How will you know your limits without an occasional failure? Never quit. Your turn will come.

Og Mandino. 60.

Choices for Successful Living

Our life is filled with choices,
Some easy and some hard.
The choice to live authentically
We never should discard.
That choice requires humility,
Sometimes bending to obey.
That choice requires willingness
To try a different way.
If we choose to live authentically
We must know ourselves quite well.
Through our own mistakes and blunders,
In time we will excel.
The treasures of that choice are ours,
Though there is a price to pay.
Yet the riches of that choice are great
As we live a different way.

Helen S. Peterson

Hopelessness

When You Seem to Be Drifting through Life . . .
Consider that which is lovely!

Five months after my precious second husband had died, I took a short cruise to the Bahamas. It was not a trip that I would ordinarily choose to take because I don't really enjoy the tropical temperatures. But, since I was struggling with getting back into life, I thought it might help to be with friends on a short vacation. I was really at loose ends at the time in life—sort-of drifting with not much direction. In my life I had experienced this sort of feeling before: when my dad died, when first husband died, and when brother died. I was aware that it would end in time, but at the time it was not a real pleasant passage. But, it was a part of life that most of us will experience at one time or another. I told myself that I would really be glad when this existence on earth was over because we would no longer have to experience losses and grief. I also told myself time heals. God heals. We heal.

It might seem impossible that when you are drifting along with no direction for anything lovely to be gained. Yet as I thought about my condition, my aimlessness, my loneliness, my unfulfilled dreams, I realized that I was still alive. I still had the opportunity to try new things in life. I still had within me the power to make choices that could break this cycle. I had time to contribute to the world things that I might not have been able to contribute had I still been happily married and settled in a comfortable place in life.

The best things in life seem to happen to all of us, whether animals, plants, humans, when our little "worlds" become disheveled. Plants that have become overpopulated die unless they are uprooted and replanted. Baby eagles would never soar unless their parents made the nest so uncomfortable that they had to get out on their own. Humans have the tendency to settle into familiar patterns unless, we too, are "uprooted" or pushed out of the nest. So, it happens that when life gets uncomfortable for us, we have the choice to live and soar, or to fight it and struggle until we die or become so weak that we no longer are able to make healthy choices. The lovely part of this time of grief, this drifting, this unpleasant passage is that once we are forced to find a new course, we actually flourish. Thank God for the passages that make us grow. Thank God that we can still make healthy choices.

Finding a Different Way

I find it is so hard to go,
And just as hard to stay.
Maybe in the future,
It will be a different way.

It's difficult to be alone.
There's no comfort in a crowd.
The noise of life is deafening.
The silence is so loud.

Life today is not the same
As days that you once knew.
And memories of times gone by,
Have changed since I've lost you.

I fear that if I lose the pain,
My love for you might die.
I need to know that I can heal—
That it's all right to try.

Will it hurt you if I choose to live
And laugh and love again?
I need to know my living life
Will never cause you pain.

I'm so confused with life today.
Don't know where I belong.
Our friends are always needing me,
But, I barely get along.

Will this painful time soon end?
I just live day by day.
Surely life will change again
If I learn a different way.

Helen S. Peterson

When You Feel as though Your Life Is on Hold . . .
Consider that which is lovely!

Some days you may wake up and wonder where you are going in life. Although you may have a regular routine, you may find that at the end your day you feel as though you have accomplished nothing. Some days you may resent having to meet new challenges or even to complete old ones. You may feel extreme agitation because you allow your friends to keep you so busy that you really don't have time to reflect or to reorganize your life. Your job may seem overwhelming or boring. Or it may be just the opposite: you may close your friends out of your life and refuse to move ahead toward the future. Regardless of the circumstances, the bottom line is that you feel as though your life is on hold and that you will never have a clear idea of where you are headed in the future.

The lovely part of this dilemma is that you are quite normal if this state lasts for a short while. Every person who experiences the loss of a loved one also goes through a time of feeling as though they are in a state of inertia. Further, these times require you to exercise your faith or to lose hope altogether. As you exercise faith and believe that your Heavenly Father knows what you are experiencing, you then develop a hope for better days ahead. A delightful example of one who had to really exercise faith when he felt his life was on hold was good old Moses. After living in luxury for forty years as the "grandson" of the Pharaoh, he grieved many losses when he found himself secluded on the backside of the desert, working with the common folk for another forty years. Although he got to know his biological family, it is quite possible that his brothers and sisters may have even shunned him for a time because of the easy life that he had prior to returning home after murdering an Egyptian man. The fact that he stuttered didn't make it any easier for him to blend in. No doubt he had to work with the animals, learning how to care for them. As a son of royalty, dear old Moses never had to dirty his hands with common labor. Good old Mo didn't really even know how to be Jewish. After all, he had grown up in an Egyptian culture surrounded by the beliefs of the Egyptian people. He had the hard task of learning the Jewish culture as an adult. You can imagine that he wondered if his life would ever have real meaning or purpose again.

But, all the loss and all the grieving and all the waiting did serve a purpose. Finally he was prepared for the real mission that God had in mind for him. That task was to lead an entire nation out of slavery and into a brand new land. It wasn't an easy job, and perhaps at times he wished he were back "on hold" again. But, because of the period of time that God used to train him, he knew how to manage "herds" of cantankerous people. In addition, he had learned how to depend upon God. That knowledge proved invaluable while wandering around in the desert with several million people for forty years.

So, never give up hope. God is working His plan for you. You may feel suspended for a time, but God is too wise to waste valuable talent. It won't be long before you will be going again if you are willing to learn from Him and to join in His work here on earth.

> "'For I know the plans I have for you,' declares the Lord, 'plans to prosper you and not to harm you, plans to give you hope and a future.'"
> -Jeremiah 29:11 (NIV)

A Place for Me to Fill

There is a place that I must fill,
A task meant just for me.
There is a work that I must do
That only I can see.

There is a word that I must speak
To cheer a dear one on.
There is a poem I must write
To bring to life a song.

There are steps that I must take
Along the road of life,
Those kindly words that I must speak
To clear away the strife.

There are flowers I must plant
To spread the beauty 'round.
There are weeds that I must pull
To hallow treasured ground.

There are tears to wipe away
From babes and others, too.
There are burdens I can share
To foster life anew.

There's a place that I can fill
And with God's help I can.
There is a special place for me
Within God's perfect plan.

Helen S. Peterson

When Healing Is Slow . . .
Consider that which is lovely!

    Many times you will become discouraged along the journey to recovery. You may think and feel as though nothing is happening to remove the pain that you experience. Oh yes, there are some days that are better than others, but for the most part, you still seem to float around without a good sense of direction for your life and sometimes wonder if there really is meaning for you here on this earth. You get so tired, and you are so lonely without someone to love you in a special way. You are confused as to who you are, and you find it hard to believe that it will ever get any better. Yet, as you look at others who have lost their loved ones, it appears that somehow they have made the transition to a new and different life. They seem to be happy.

    It is hard to realize that even though you see and feel no changes in yourself, subtle changes are taking place. It is much like what happens to a beautiful daffodil or tulip bulb. In the fall of the year you plant it deep in the dark soil. Then it must be exposed to some very cold, perhaps even freezing temperatures for a period of time or else it will not generate the cells needed to grow in the spring. Even while the snow lies on top of the ground, the bulb is changing within. After the appropriate period of time, it begins to show signs of life. Yet, the first life that you see is not the beautiful flower. Instead, tiny green shoots come out of the dark ground. Sometimes they are still hidden by the snow or the leaves that have fallen upon it. After a long while, during which time the bulb continues to use the nutrients that have been stored within, the buds pop out of the ground. When the warm sunshine of late winter or early spring begins to permeate the soil, the bud gradually unfolds with a staggering beauty for the world to behold.

    Consider it lovely that you are now in that stage of rest, waiting for the springtime of your grief. Consider it lovely that although you cannot see or feel what is happening, new life is developing. Believe that your Creator knows and sees. He has already provided you with the nutrients that you will need to begin to grow again and to blossom into a new person. Consider that as you go through the darkness and cold of winter, changes are taking place. You are regaining the strength that you need to make that transition out of darkness and cold into the warmth of the sunlight. Consider it lovely that when you have come into full bloom again, you will be a beautiful object because you have gone through the darkness, pain, and isolation of your loss. Consider it wonderful that when you are once again a healed person, you will be able to encourage others as they encounter grief.

"See! The winter is past; the rains are over and gone.
Flowers appear on the earth; the season of singing has come,
the cooing of doves is heard in our land."
-Song of Solomon 2:11–12 (NIV)

After the Storms Are Gone

The storm clouds are gone.
Now comes the light.
Daybreak most welcomed,
Follows darkness of night.

Life's rich treasures
Come to life anew
As the earth in its pleasure
Shines through the sparkling dew.

Lovely flowers peep through
The darkness of the earth.
Tiny birds now fly about
Singing songs of mirth.

Little children entranced
With insects, oh so small.
Happy faces smiling now,
Life changes for us all.

Helen S. Peterson

When You Feel Tied to the Past . . .
Consider that which is lovely!

Many times during your bereavement you may feel as though you are not making any progress toward moving on with life. Each day you may feel as though you take three steps forward and two backward. Feelings of grief may continue to swoop over you at the most unexpected times. And, at times you may feel as though you are dragging a heavy weight along with you. While all of these feelings are normal, it may also be that there are things that impede your progress toward acceptance of your loss.

On May 9, 2012, Dr. Arthur Caliandro, Senior Minister of Marble Collegiate Church in New York City, preached a sermon entitled *"On Letting Go."* In his sermon he told the story of how he got into his little raft one day to row from his island home to the shore. The wind was blowing and the water was a little rough. He rowed and rowed, working himself into a bit of exhaustion but making no progress. He assumed that the wind and waves were just too strong for his little raft. Suddenly from the shore a young lad yelled to him "Arthur, untie the raft." Much to his chagrin, he realized that he was still tied to the mooring that had held the raft from drifting away. Caliandro. Sermon in Marble Collegiate Church.

Dr. Caliandro wanted us to realize no matter how old or wise we are, sometimes we are tied to situations, events, things, or people that keep us from moving on in a successful manner. Perhaps you are still tied to old habits, old expectations, and old attitudes that keep you moored to the past. Perhaps you have anger or sorrow that keeps you tied securely to the moor. Perhaps you have made assumptions about being unable to move against or through this difficult time in your life. Maybe it is time for self-examination to find some causes in your life to help you understand why you are unable to move ahead through the waters of grief and bereavement.

It is emancipating to take the time for introspection to learn what may impel you ahead or impede your progress forward. Growth is painful, and letting go of some old thinking and behavior may be hard. Letting go of things of the past doesn't mean that you are giving up. In fact, it is just the opposite. It means that you are accepting that things can never be the same and that you have a new way to go now. From the time you were an infant, you grasped on to things and held on dearly as though letting go might be detrimental. But when you were able to let go, you enjoyed new freedom. The joy of letting of the past and moving on is that you realize you are, indeed, a very strong person with hope for a good future.

The sheer joy of discovering those hidden roadblocks and moorings gives freedom to move forward in a new and exciting way. Only when you are willing to be honest about your feelings and your attitudes do you make real progress. That is evidence of movement toward maturity and toward a new life with emotional health and joy. How lovely it is to find you are no longer tied to the past.

St. Paul was an Orthodox Jew. He was a member of the Sanhedrin. He held great status within the Jewish community. Of all who persecuted Christians, he was one of the most ardent. Yet, God took away all of that. Quite possibly he also took away his family, but we are never really told about them. Yet, when he realized that he must have a new life, he wrote the following:

> "One thing I do: Forgetting what is behind and straining toward what is ahead, I press on toward the goal to win the prize for which God has called me heavenward in Christ Jesus."
> -Philippians 3:13–14 (NIV)

Paul had grieved his losses. He had remained out of the mainstream of the community for about thirteen or fourteen years. But, when God told him that he had a new plan for his life, Paul began the days of preparation and eventually was able to evangelize the entire known world at the time. Because of his willingness to believe God, we are all blessed today.

Who knows? Perhaps you are the next instrument that God is preparing for his great work in this world.

When You Feel as If Life Is Meaningless . . .
Consider that which is lovely!

You are now alone. The meaning of your life has changed. Perhaps you have spent months, even years, caring for your loved one. Now he or she is deceased. Your focus has been to care for that person or to care about that person constantly. Perhaps you have remained in your career, and now you second-guess if that was selfish of you because the meaning and the joy seem to be gone. You see no real future for yourself apart from the one you loved. Perhaps you did not have a career, and your function was to provide the care that was needed on an everyday basis. Now what do you do?

How can you go on? How can you now conjure up hope and purpose for yourself? The famous violinist Itzhak Perlman had an experience that can inspire each of us. During a concert at Lincoln Center in New York City in 1975, this unique and courageous man made his way on to the stage, walking on the crutches that had been his aid since a bout with childhood polio. After unclasping the braces so that he could bend his knees, he signaled to the conductor to begin the concert. But as he played the beautiful notes on his violin, suddenly he stopped. A string on his violin had snapped. He sat for a moment with his head down, the audience wondering what he would do. In a few seconds he signaled to the conductor to continue with the concert while he played on a violin with a missing string. Throughout the music he mentally transposed each note and chord, as he needed to.

At the end of the concert, the audience briefly sat in rapt silence and then broke out into the most enthusiastic applause of his career. At the end of the applause, Perlman spoke softly and calmly. "You know, sometimes it is the artist's task to find out how much music you can still make with what you have left."

Perhaps it is now time for you to find out how much music you can still make with what you have left. You may have to stop what you are doing for a short while so that you can regroup your resources. You may have to diligently seek God's wisdom. But, you will likely be extremely surprised as you reach out to others and find new purposes for your life. It may not be easy. It was not easy for Perlman to transpose the notes at the moment he was playing. It took great courage for him to try. In doing so, he reached another level of expertise and understanding of the gift that God had given to him. In working diligently in your own life to renew purpose and meaning, it will take great courage. If you try, you too will find that God has given you talents and abilities that you never knew existed. And that is what is so lovely about forging ahead, slowly, and patiently in the face of loss.

"Whatsoever you do, do all to the glory of God."
-1 Corinthians 10:31 (KJV)

The Parade

Alone—in the parade of life.
What meaning can I find
To assuage the pain within?
Alone—too dazed to know
Which way to turn.
Must I forever remain alone?
Oh! I am never completely alone.
No! I have *life* within!
I will march in that living parade.
I will find new music
To enjoy the journey until the end.

Helen S. Peterson

When You Begin to Feel Sorry for Yourself . . .
Consider that which is lovely!

Because you feel so badly about the loss that you have experienced, you sometimes begin to think that you are all alone in the world with your suffering. You become so focused on how much you hurt that you are unable to realize that others have had similar suffering and grief. It is at these times that Satan can work to discourage you and cause you to move your thoughts away from the hope that is in God.

In times when watchmen guarded the walls of the city, they could never give up their vigilance lest the enemy advance and overtake the city. Standing high on the surrounding walls, the watchmen were the first line of defense by observing any movement that might signal an advancing enemy. For the sake of their safety, they could never afford to sleep on duty. Your heart, like those cities, needs to be guarded against the advancing attacks of Satan with the walls of truth and faith and with watchfulness. Your mind or heart is like the walls of a city. Unless you are vigilant in dispelling the negative thoughts or feelings, you may be overtaken by negativism and despair.

When you have suffered a great loss in your life, you are extremely vulnerable. You tend to feel sorry for yourself and wonder why this loss has occurred to you, or perhaps so soon in life. As the shock of the loss wears off, frequently you begin to think negatively about the loss. You think things such as: "I didn't do enough to help." "If I had only gone to one more doctor . . ." "God is punishing me for the sins of the past." "God loves so and so more than He loves me because he healed her spouse, and he didn't heal my spouse." Even though these thoughts may be the result of depression or chemical deprivation at the time, Satan would like to use them to discourage you. Yes, Satan is God's enemy and he will do anything he can to "steal" you away from God. Of course, he can't, but he causes you to think thoughts of pity for yourself. If you allow yourself to get caught in this snare, your grief process will be prolonged, and you will continue to suffer much longer than is necessary.

What is lovely about knowing this? It is wonderful to know that you can call upon God in prayer. It is lovely to know that you do not have to remain in a state of self-pity if you guard your thoughts and don't let them overtake you. It is lovely to know that when you have grieved your losses, you will be strong and alert once again. It is lovely to know that Satan cannot defeat you when you are God's children. All of these thoughts give you strength to rid yourself of negative thinking of this sort and to focus on positive thoughts of being able to see your loved one again someday.

God, I know that I am vulnerable today. I know that I have been feeling sorry for myself. I do not want to be this way. I know you can help me to think more positively. Will you please help me to dispel these thoughts and replace them with your loving thoughts? Will you help me to feel your comforting arms around me today? Thank you, God. Amen.

>O LORD, You have searched me and known *me*.
>My sitting down and my rising up;
>You understand my thought afar off.
>You comprehend my path and my lying down,
>And are acquainted with all my ways.
>For *there is* not a word on my tongue,
>*But* behold, O LORD, You know it altogether.
>You have hedged me behind and before,
>And laid Your hand upon me.
>*Such* knowledge *is* too wonderful for me;
>It is high, I cannot *attain* it.
>
>-Psalm 139:1–6 (ESV)

When the Future Seems So Bleak . . .
Consider that which is lovely!

At times, during the course of your grief journey, you are bright and cheerful, thinking of nothing but the lovely day and the friends and time that you have in this life. At other times, the future seems dark and bleak. You may look ahead and think to yourself "I may have thirty or forty or fifty more years ahead on this planet. What am I going to do that is meaningful and filled with some semblance of peace and joy?" This may be the time that you can't see beyond the next hour or the next day. You may be wondering if you will ever find another spouse to love you—and, if you do, will that person support your endeavors to live out the values in which you have believed all your life. The prospect of remarriage may seem foreign or even impossible, yet you are so lonely and so without a sense of direction for your remaining years. While it may feel as though you are betraying the one who has died, it has some appeal over spending your days and nights alone.

At times such as these you may wonder if there is really any sense in your living any longer. But, you won't take your life because it would hurt too many people, and you know it is really not the right thing to do. An air of despondency sets in which is so hard to overcome, and you are tired of "bothering" people with your mourning, so you live with your pain and don't say anything to anyone.

There are some thoughts that can make this time more hopeful and more positive and lovely. Perhaps it would help you to know that Christ, Himself, felt very alone and had virtually no one to turn to except his Heavenly Father. For three years he lived and worked among people who came to be known as his friends. Yet they did not have a clue as to the anticipatory grief that he endured. When he could only foresee being forsaken by the Father in the Garden of Gethsemane, he cried out so arduously that it was as though he sweat drops of blood. In those very moments he experienced what you suffer here when you are left alone with a seemingly bleak future ahead of you. In some ways, when you go through these times, you are truly "suffering with Christ."

At the moment, it does not seem as though there is anything even remotely good to consider about these hopeless feelings. But, after the time has passed when you are feeling so deserted and useless, without purpose or plan, you begin to imagine the things that you can possibly do to make your life valid and meaningful again. Although you cannot go out and marry the first person you see on the street, you can evaluate what qualities you are missing in that wonderful spouse who is now no longer with you. You can make lists of what you might want in another person if one were to come along. You can consider what you would have wanted your spouse to do if it had been you to die instead. You can imagine the wildest things that you have ever been free to think of regarding how your life might be renewed and revitalized for whatever future you might have ahead. All of the pain that you experience tends to push you in the direction of searching and making changes. That is the blessing in this kind of despondency and seeming hopelessness. As you cling to the promises that God has given to you, you regain the strength to actually believe those promises and to help them to happen. You must remember that God only wants what is best for you and that He has promised to meet your needs and grant the desires of your heart if you are in tune with Him.

> "'For I know the plans that I have for you,' declares the Lord. 'They are plans to prosper you and not to harm you, plans to give you hope and a future. Then you will call upon me and come and pray to me, and I will listen to you. You will find me when you seek me with all your heart.'"
>
> -Jeremiah 33:11–14 (NIV)

Lessons We Can Learn

I hear the birds chirping on this lovely bright morn.
Their sound is delightful as they join in a song.
It seems they are joyful gathering food for the day,
Saying thanks to their Maker in their own unique way.

The butterflies, too, have begun flitting around,
Gathering nectar from flowers, with never a sound.
They seem so pleased with each morsel they find
As they dance from my view, leaving pleasure behind.

Bees are now buzzing all about
A hive in a housetop from which they come out.
Right now there are far too many to count.
The number of them has started to mount.

They move very quickly as they care for the hive,
Gathering food for the queen to keep her alive.
They all do their tasks in methodical way
And busily work throughout the long day.

It seems we can learn from these friends in our view
That life is quite busy, there's so much to do.
So when you feel hopeless, despondent and alone,
Remember these creatures, and join in their song.

Though their work is so meager and seemingly drone
They have great value on earth as they carry on.

Helen S. Peterson

"We do not measure life by the number of breaths we take, but by the moments that take our breath away."
-Author unknown

When One Day Runs into the Next . . .
Consider that which is lovely!

After my spouse died, I decided to discontinue my professional career for a while to allow myself to heal and become the new person that God was helping me to become. I said this to a colleague, and of course, I thought she would immediately affirm my "wise" decision. Instead she replied: "But, how will you punctuate your time?" Although I was a bit taken back at her rather forthright question, I thought it was a good question and one that has great meaning to those of us who are widowed, whether we are gainfully employed or not.

Basically, she was referring to having some way to feel a sense of completion or fulfillment with what you have done with your time in any given day. If you do not have some sort of schedule to live by, either time just seems to drag laboriously from one day to the next giving you no real hope or no reason to look ahead, or time just slips away and you feel as though you have accomplished nothing worthwhile. Your intentions may have been good, but at the end of the day you feel as though you have done nothing but grieve. "Punctuating" one's time is a valuable aspect of life, and one that you do if you follow a regular routine from day to day. But when you live in the state of a mental daze that grief seems to engender, it is often hard to have rhyme and reason to your life. It is best if you have regular routines that you follow. Even though it does help to organize your life, sometimes it is still difficult to focus. Instead of becoming stuck and muddling around in a maze, how can you make this a meaningful time of your life and one that has lovely outcomes?

During this very confusing period of your life, you can become a much more mature and patient individual. It is a time when you can learn what your priorities really need to be in order to survive life in this very complex world. You can evaluate what you need to or want to do and then make some good decisions about what you are really able to do with the time and energy that you have. By such evaluation you can then try to accomplish one or more things that will punctuate your day. However, if you allow frustration with your current circumstances to creep into your thinking, you will certainly rob yourself of the positive energy that you need to heal. But, if you quietly accept this time as a part of the healing process, you can gain peace about the many changes that are happening. By setting one or two goals to accomplish each day, you gain a sense of control over your life. What is important is to recognize that even something as simple as getting out of bed and getting dressed can be a major accomplishment some days. No goal attained is too small or too insignificant when you are struggling to get your bearings in life again.

By choosing to move outside of your comfort zones you can begin to see other ways how you might take control of your life. Deliberately choosing to go out with friends or family may be very tiring, but it will help to punctuate your time as you schedule the event and then prepare for it. Signing up for a class at a local college or YMCA may also be a way of deliberately making you punctuate your time. When you have to meet your commitment, then you are forced to move outside your own little world into the larger world in which you must continue to live.

The lovely thing about having some sort of schedule that you must follow is that it gives you tiny goals that you must achieve. As you achieve each small goal, you gradually gain a sense of being whole again. You gain a sense of control over your life as you set that schedule and then work to fulfill it. At the end of each day, you are able to look back over the time spent and know that something good was accomplished even though it may have taken every ounce of strength that you had for that day. Of course, learning to schedule your time is great discipline long after you have moved beyond your grief.

Father God,

Time is so precious and yet I don't know how to make it work for me. Either I struggle with time that passes too slowly or I wonder where time has gone. I don't like that my life is so uncoordinated now. I don't enjoy the feelings of being lost and confused that I have so frequently. I don't want to go on for my whole life in this manner. Please help me to find some things to make life meaningful again. Please help me to learn how to set some simple goals that I may achieve in order to use the time that I have in this world in a wise and orderly fashion. If I do not have purpose and goals I will lose hope. Thank you for guiding me. Amen.

Life Is a Bridge

Life is a bridge over which we all must cross.
To make it to safety, we must juggle the burdens of loss.
Life is a forest through which we all must fare.

We must heed the marks left by those before us there.
Life is an ocean of deep dark waters to either float or swim.
To traverse those waters of murky demure,
Our strength must come from within.
Life is a journey up mountainside and into ravine below.
Courage and hope that come from God are what will help us go.
Life is a question of endless debate filled with faith and fear,
The going is often uncertain, and the end is not so clear.
Life has days filled with rain, but then the sun will shine.
For each of us it is different, created by God's design.
So if your life is hard today, know that the Creator cares.
He will help to see you through and wipe away your tears.
Yes, Life is a bridge over which we all must cross.
To make it to safety we must juggle the burdens of loss.

Helen S. Peterson

When You Are Too Close to See . . .
Consider that which is lovely!

In the Louvre in Paris there is a hall where the Mona Lisa hangs. Although she is placed high enough to stand right beneath her and not do any damage to the awesome painting, there is a railing around the piece of art that keeps people at a distance. This is not so much for protection, but rather for perspective. If you were to stand just beneath and look up, you would only see fine brush strokes and a myriad of darkened colors. But, standing at a distance and walking from side to side, the painting actually comes to life as the famous lady's eyes seem to follow you from spot to spot.

So it is with your life right now. You are here in the midst of grief. It seems to you that you are making no progress toward accepting your loss and "moving on." Each day seems to be the same even though months have gone by. Waves of sadness still seem to envelop you at times. It continues to be hard to make some decisions, and your world still seems very abnormal.

Yet, from the perspective of others who see you from a distance, they see that you have made so many steps forward. They see that you are getting out and doing things that are good for you. They see you smiling and laughing and genuinely enjoying yourself at times. They might even envy the progress that you are making, thinking that they could not have done what you are doing.

The process of recovery from grief is best viewed from a distance. It is simply too big to see where it ends when you are standing and looking up at it. It seems to go on forever. Because it seems to be endless and because it is too hard to see your own progress, it is easy to become despondent and wonder if God has forsaken you. Because it hurts, sometimes a feeling of hopelessness sets in.

Consider it wonderful that God is so close to you that He actually sees and feels your pain. He sees the end to your suffering, and He walks the pathway with you to the end. Consider it lovely that as you move through your grief, you are growing, even though you do not realize it. As a child, you may have experienced growing pains in your body. You couldn't see the growth, but one day you were able to do things that you had not been able to do before. As you go through the growing pains of grief, know that you are becoming a stronger and more mature individual. You are learning that being able to ask for help is not a weakness. You are finding it easier to share your pain, and you are learning that most humans feel things that you do. Consider it lovely that as you grow in compassion, you are becoming a more genuine person, free from so many of the "masks" that you had lived with for so long. Consider it a rich blessing that you can be one of those persons who understands loss and suffering in a new way and that you can be a source of inspiration to others who will still walk the path.

> "Even though I walk through the valley of the shadow of death, I will fear no evil, for you are with me; your rod and your staff, they comfort me."
>
> -Psalm 23:4 (NIV)

When You Feel as though Your Time Is Wasted . . .
Consider that which is lovely!

When you are grieving the loss of a loved one, some days may seem to be entirely wasted. You may not feel as though you can accomplish a thing of any value. It is a chore to get out of bed, and another chore to get bathed and dressed for the day. Some days you may not even make it that far. This may especially be true once the protection of the shock reaction has worn off and you are experiencing your sorrow with no way to shield you from it.

It may be that you wander aimlessly about the house or drive aimlessly about in the car. At work you may find yourself suddenly overwhelmed by grief and unable to complete the tasks at hand. On these days, life may seem to be very laborious and very dreary. Even though the sun may be shining, you may be drooping inside. Take heart, these days generally happen to everyone who grieves.

As you go through these days, you will notice that under normal grief conditions, they do not last forever. Soon you will begin to notice that there is very little in life that is permanent. Just as times of great joy or happiness only last a short while, so it is with times of deep grief and mourning. Everything has a beginning and an end. That is how it is with human life. As you become mindful of how life is continually changing, even under pleasant conditions, you will gain hope and an ability to endure the unpleasant feelings of being immobilized by grief.

So, what could possibly be lovely about a situation in which you feel useless, tired, disinterested, and lost? One thing that is lovely is that you learn to look at life more realistically. You learn to appreciate the fact that joy, as well as sorrow, has its limit. Thus you enjoy that which is present and endure that which is not, knowing it all will change with time.

Further, it is not so much how you feel that is important. Feelings are transient and often incorrect. Feelings are strongly related to chemical processes in your body. Today the chemicals are not operating at their prime. Perhaps it will be a time for you to learn how to help your body maintain a better balance of chemistry by eating properly and exercising in moderation. These can be lovely outcomes of the distress that you feel during these emotional "shut downs." There is a good chance that by tomorrow your chemicals will be restored to a better balance and you will feel more like living.

In the interim, your body is resting from physical labor because you don't feel like doing anything. That is a good thing. The emotional stress of your loss has depleted your body of the nutrients that it needs to live properly, and you really need rest. Further, "down time" allows your mind to slowly process your loss and help you to make the transition to a new normal way of life. Such changes take place slowly and in isolation from other distractions. That, too, is a good thing.

In nature, when things are out of balance, the tendency is to try to bring them back into balance. Because these feelings are uncomfortable, something within you will seek to get beyond them and back into balance. Within the body, we say that we are attaining homeostasis. Lamenting that you cannot do today what you used to be able to do only tends to discourage you. But there is value and beauty in doing your best today, whatever that best may be. Babies take baby steps, often hanging on to something as they move forward. There is loveliness in moving ahead taking baby steps. As you see the results of those tiny steps, they soon become large accomplishments. You can appreciate that each step taken forward is one more little movement toward good emotional and spiritual health. You may find yourself courageously beginning a new hobby or activity. Perhaps you may even decide to attend a support group where you find others who are also dealing with similar feelings. These things are good and will begin the process of new life for you.

Never consider these times as wasted time. Seldom is a great masterpiece completed in just one day. Your life is a masterpiece. It will take a little time to make it the beautiful life that it will be. Although the Master is in charge, the part that remains for you is to help the process by caring for yourself physically and by allowing yourself to be molded or made into whatever He chooses to make it into. Join Him in His work.

Grieving Normally

Some days I ride a roller coaster going up and down.
Some days I ride a bicycle scooting 'round the town.
Some days I ride on roller skates and take a sudden fall.
Some days I simply stay in bed and do nothing at all.
Some days I feel as though I can win any race I desire.
Some days I feel as though I have a very flat tire.
I thought this time was wasted as I journeyed through my grief.
But now I know 'twas normal, and that brings me great relief.

Helen S. Peterson

When You Have No Motivation . . .
Consider that which is lovely!

During your time of bereavement, sometimes you know there is so much to do; yet you just don't feel like doing anything at all. You spend time on mindless tasks never really completing any of them, thus engendering a sense of guilt because you are wasting time. Your ability to concentrate on the task at hand is so short that sometimes you just give up or become irritable. If you have go to work and don't accomplish that which you should be accomplishing, you fear you may get fired. If you are at home, you fear that life will never get any better, so you allow yourself to slip into a feeling of desolation or desperation. You go through the motions of your everyday tasks, but often you neglect to do even those, until your environment becomes cluttered and chaotic, thus adding to your sense of loss. Life just seems to have no reason or rhyme. Even though the sun may be shining outdoors, it is gloom and doom within.

What could possibly be lovely about having these feelings? Do you remember the words of Psalm 23? It says, "You make me lie down in green pastures. You restore my soul." During this time, when you are working through your grief and such feelings occur, it is well to consider what it meant for a shepherd to make his sheep lie down in green pastures. Sheep are not very smart animals. If they were to have their own way about things, they would just wander about, always munching on whatever they could find to eat, and even wandering off from the safety of the shepherd and the rest of the herd. Thereby they would become more susceptible to attack by other animals, and eventually would lose their lives. When the shepherd knows his sheep should rest, he gently places his hand on the head of the lead sheep, and pushes it down to the ground. Soon the others will follow, and very soon all will rest. If they need to obtain sustenance, they easily have access to it because a good shepherd brings his sheep to a place where the eating is easy and to where waters flow quietly so that the sheep will not be afraid to drink from them.

God is your shepherd. Therefore, as you consider this time of your life, think of it as a time when he made you "lie down in green pastures." Soon the time will come when your mission will resume. You will be alert and active again. But, for now, God wants you to be at rest. Do what you have to do. Do what you are able to do, and don't fault yourself for what you are unable to do or unwilling to do at this time. Consider it a lovely time in life that God has provided for you to restore your soul and to become ready for the next mission that He is planning for you. Remember that it is far better to treasure what you have today than to immerse yourself in grieving over that which you have lost.

> "God is our refuge and strength, a very present help in trouble."
> -Psalm 46:1 (KJV)

Psalm Twenty-Three

The Lord is my shepherd, I shall not want.
He makes me lie down in green pastures.
He leads me beside still waters;

He restores my soul.
He leads me in paths of righteousness for His name's sake.

Even though I walk through the valley of the shadow of death,
I fear no evil; for thou art with me;
thy rod and thy staff, they comfort me.

Thou preparest a table before me in the presence of my enemies;
thou anointest my head with oil, my cup overflows.

Surely goodness and mercy shall follow me all the days of my life;
and I shall dwell in the house of the LORD forever.

-Psalm 23 (RSV)

When Times Are "Awful" and You Are Discouraged . . .
Consider that which is lovely!

When you are grieving, you sometimes have a really, really *bad* day. You know, the kind of day when you get up in the morning and you have forgotten to dry the wash, so your favorite shirt is still in the washer and you can't wear it as you had planned? Then you go to take your shower and the showerhead has become clogged with mineral deposits so that half of it isn't spraying? And when you go to get milk for your cereal that you are making yourself eat even though you are not hungry, you discover that someone else has just used up all the milk? Finally, you get into your car, already late for your day, and realize you completely forgot to get gas last night so you'll have to stop on your way to your destination? Now that's the beginning of a very bad day. But terrible, horrible, no good, very bad days happen even in Australia!

The rest of the day is spent solving one challenge after another until you go home exhausted from your very bad day. Some days are like this, even though you are doing your best to move ahead in life.

What can you do in the face of such a day? How can you make it better?

Well, the command of God is: "This is the day that the Lord has made, let us rejoice and be glad in it" (Psalm 118:24, ESV). What? God made this awful day for you? Thanks God. Could you please bless someone else with this day, please, please?

Yes! By trying to think of things for which you can rejoice, you change your mindset from the negative to the positive. You can see what is lovely and perhaps even humorous in this day. Having a lot of things go wrong naturally sets you up for negative thinking. So, instead of remaining in that frame of mind, if you choose to think about positive things, then you begin to see positive things. Wayne Dyer, one of America's motivational speakers, has given us a good thought: "If you change the way you look at things, the things you look at change." Wayne Dyer..

It is true. When you choose to look at a situation and search for the good in it, then the good becomes more obvious and the bad seems to fade into the background. At the end of what you have perceived as a very bad day, if you can say, "It was a day full of challenges, most of which I overcame." then you have mastered the concept of changing the way you look at things.

Another way of changing your perception of "bad" events is to keep from fretting. Fretting is time spent mulling over a situation and taking no action to ameliorate it or see it from a different perspective. It is a waste of our precious time because it brings no positive result. Many people will say they are going to pray about things. That is wonderful if in your prayers you truly relinquish the bad events to God's keeping. The trouble with our prayers is that often we don't give up our fretting. Rather, we just complain to God about how things are. So, if you are going to pray, then you must also let go of the fretting and set the events aside so that God has a chance to work out the solutions that are necessary.

Still another way to deal with a day that has multiple challenges is to extract yourself from the familiar environment in which you generally function. Taking a walk in the park during lunchtime, reading an interesting novel, going to the mall for lunch, going outside in the yard, or calling a friend and making plans for the weekend all become ways to extract yourself from the normal environment in which you function. Each activity that is different helps to infuse your soul with hope. Hope is that entity that helps you to go on living and believing that things will change—that they will get better with time.

In *Anne of Green Gables* written by Lucy Maude Montgomery in 1908, Anne talks with her "mother" about some mistakes that she has made and about her discouragement for the future. Anne then says to her mother: "Isn't it nice to think that tomorrow is a new day with no mistakes in it yet?" Montgomery. Chapter 21.

This such a wonderful way to realize that when you are able to rest, away from the situations that plague you, you will awaken to a new day, with no wrinkles in it. In the quietness of rest, your mind is better able to sort through the details that trouble you and come to some logical conclusions. Such hope inspires you to go on with renewed vigor.

Yet another way in which you can come to rejoice in your very bad day is to take a good long walk and let your body become invigorated from the exercise. When you feel better physically, when you let go of some of the tension that bad days bring with them, then you feel lighter and better able to function. Things don't seem quite as bad because you have taken control over your day, at least in part.

The reason why you often perceive things as bad in your day is because you feel out of control of events. The sensible thing to do is for you to take some control of that which you are able to control, and just accept that "change happens." Gracefully accepting that life is filled with unexpected events is a wonderful way in which to deal with all those things that seem to be bad. If you expect the unexpected, then you aren't taken aback by it when it happens.

Whatever happens to you to this day, face the challenges with optimism and with grace. Go on putting one foot in front of the other and continue to believe that

God walks beside you, aware of anything that you cannot bear. At those times, you will know He is caring for you as He guides you through the valley of the Shadow of Death and places you once again in green pastures.

"There are good days and there are bad days, and this is one of them!"
Lawrence Welk.

When You Wonder If God Really Has a Plan for You . . .
Consider that which is lovely!

It is very hard to believe that God really cares about you or about your future when you are struggling with the loss of a loved one. Frequently, you lose hope when you are in the midst of confusion or emotional chaos. Because you feel desolate and uncertain about your future without your loved one, you wonder if God is even there, and if He is, does he really understand your confusion? Does He really have a plan for your life?

No doubt, when Joseph was abandoned by his brothers and sent to Egypt to live, he must have felt that the situation was hopeless and futile. No doubt, he grieved greatly the loss of his relationship with his dad and even with some of the brothers. For years he may have struggled with whether there really was a plan or if God really understood the loss that he had experienced. But one day, long after he had been abandoned, God revealed to him the secrets of His marvelous plan. Not only had God worked out the plan to reunite Joseph with his brothers and father, but there was an even greater plan. That greater plan was to allow this little family to grow in seclusion into a large nation known as the Children of God. Joseph may never have realized the role he played during his lifetime, but God knew what He was doing in allowing Joseph to endure the losses that he did for the greater good of a nation.

When you doubt that God really has a plan for your life now that you are feeling so alone and abandoned, consider it lovely that you must exercise your faith in God and become strong by depending solely upon Him to work out the details of your life. Of course, you have your job to do, but ultimately, it is He who is working the plan that He can see from a vantage far greater than yours or mine. Perhaps even today you should journal your doubts so that when the larger plan is revealed, you will see that God indeed is in control of your days and that His ultimate purpose for allowing you to suffer the loss that you have has been so much greater than you could ever imagine.

> "The Lord is good, a refuge in times of trouble. He cares for those who trust in him."
>
> -Nahum 1:7 (NIV)

If God Is Real

If God is real, then where was He
When my heart was broken with pain?
If God is real, why didn't He hear
As I called out again and again?

If God is real, then why did He abandon me?
Why did He let evil have its way?
Why didn't He come with His mighty power
And rescue me that day?

I was tormented and torn in two.
Didn't he see the damage done?
Didn't he hear my screaming heart?
Or did He look away with scorn?

My Child, though you couldn't see,
I didn't abandon you.
I carried you gently in my arms
As the fire and floods went through.

I was there with you while you suffered with me.
I cried tears as evil worked its pain,
Your broken heart is in my hands
And I will heal it once again.

My child, don't you know that I made a promise to you?
My child, do you believe that what I say is true?
I promised I would never leave, nor forsake that which I own.
You are my child, my precious one; I will never leave you alone.

Helen S. Peterson

When Faith Is All You Have Left . . .
Consider that which is lovely!

During my years of counseling, I heard about some sad and difficult situations. The story about Lea (names and locations have been changed) is a true one and indicative of how, when we hang on to faith, we are able to keep on living, successfully.

Lea sat shocked, gazing dumbly at the television screen before her. While watching the evening news she learned that her precious husband was dead. The shock was so great that she sat in disbelief, not wanting to hear what her ears had told her was true. Later, when the Military Police came to tell her about her husband's death, she was barely able to speak to them.

Lea, of Asian descent, had come to the United States with her military husband. Although they had been married for many years, the couple had no children. In those years they had become each other's best friend, confidante, advisor, and lover. In the months following Charlie's death, Lea was faced with the dilemma of trying to extract from the Criminal Investigation Division of the United States Army whether they believed his death was a homicide or a suicide since it happened on an active military base in the middle of the day while he was on duty. The cause of death would determine whether she would receive an insurance remuneration or not.

Lea felt alone and terrified. She had no immediate family in the United States to help her bear the grief of her husband's death. Further, she had no source of income since she had always been a homemaker for her husband and herself. Her command of the language was adequate, but she had no education or experience to enable her to find a job. She soon spent the little bit of money the couple had saved paying the monthly house mortgage, car payments, utilities, and other normal expenses of living. But after that, no money came in since the CID could not issue a death certificate as to the nature of the death. Without the death certificate no insurance payments could be made to her. Fortunately, both Lea and her husband had developed a strong belief in God, and a sincere faith that God will care for His children as they live out their missions here on earth. Through the fall and winter months, Lea diligently prayed that God would provide for her financial needs so that she would not lose her house or her car. Amazingly, in ways that she does not know, the death insurance was settled even without a death certificate, enabling her to pay the mortgage and car loan.

As holidays approached and she was alone and despondent, she prayed that God would use her in some magnificent way. One day she saw a notice that volunteers were needed to serve dinner to hundreds of homeless ladies in a local shelter on Christmas Day. Having no family, she volunteered. That day, she began a new life! She went from being by herself—alone, sad and afraid—to being with four hundred very grateful women who appreciated her and loved her for her service to them. From that day she continues to work with the ladies, encouraging them, witnessing to them, and reaching out in love. The blessings of giving selflessly in the midst of her grief and loneliness have come pouring into her life. While she still suffers tremendous pain from her loss, and the cause of Charlie's death has not yet been resolved, God has enlarged her vision and made her life bearable as she lives through her pain on the way to healing.

The loss that Lea experienced brought her to the lowest valley of her life. Looking up from that valley, she saw that her only way out was to trust in God to give her wisdom, strength, and courage. God did more than that for her. He rewarded her faith and dependence on Him by providing her the means to pay for her house and vehicle. He brought her into a huge family of "sisters," all of whom love her and care about the pain that she feels. And most precious of all, she has learned that when one completely yields his or her life to Him, surely God will provide in wonderful and marvelous ways. Lea has not completed her walk through the Valley of the Shadow of Death, but as she walks, she holds the hand of her precious Savior, knowing that as she needs to rest from the pain, He certainly will lead her "beside the stilled waters."

When your pain seems unbearable and your fear seems to overwhelm you, remember that all God really wants is for you to depend on Him. He created you to have a loving relationship with Him. He will show you the way to do the rest. That is what is lovely about being alone, destitute, and despondent. When you reach out, you will find love, wisdom, and a means of healing.

> "Trust in the Lord with all your heart, and lean not on your own understanding; in all your ways acknowledge him and he will make your paths straight."
>
> -Proverbs 3:5-6 (NIV)

Bibliography

Blackaby, Henry T.. Created to Be God's Friend: How God Shapes Those He Loves. Nashville: Thomas Nelson, Inc., 1999. 48.

Bombeck, Erma. *Eat Less Cottage Cheese and More Ice Cream: Thoughts on Life.* Kansas City, MO: Andrews McMeel Publishing, 1979, 2003. Text originally appeared in a newspaper column, "*If I Had My Life to Live Over.*" December 2, 1979.

Browning, Robert. "Along the Road" cited in Edith P. Hazen, ed., The Columbia Granger's Index to Poetry, 10th edition. New York: Columbia University Press, 1993.

Dartt, Tracey. *God on the Mountain*. Spring House Productions Inc. c.2005. Sung by Lynda Randle. Compact Disc manufactured by Gaither Music Group, Alexandria, IN.

Frank, Anne. *The Diary of a Young Girl. February 23, 1944.* Translated from the Dutch by B.M. Mooyart- Doubleday. New York: Doubleday, A division of Random House, Inc. 1967.

Harry Emerson Fosdick . BrainyQuote.com, Xplore Inc, 2015. http//www.brainyquote.com/quotes/quotes/h/harryemers377865.html, accessed May 20, 2015

Johnson, Ph.D. Lynn D. *Enjoy Life! Healing with Happiness.* Salt Lake City, Utah: Head Acre Press, 2008.

Lawrence Welk. BrainyQuote.com, Xplore Inc, 2015. http://www.brainyquote.com/quotes/quotes/l/lawrencewe383759.html, accessed May 20, 2015.

Lewis, C.S. *A Grief Observed*. United Kingdom: Faber and Faber, 1961.

Lindburgh, Anne Morrow. *Hour of Gold, Hour of Lead: Diaries and Letters of Anne Morrow Lindbergh. 1973.* New York: Houghton Mifflin Harcourt, 1993.

Mandino , Og. *A Better Way to Live: Og Mandino's Own Personal Story of Success.* New York: Bantam Books, Bantam Doubleday Dell Publishing Group, 1970.

Montgomery, Lucy Maude. *Anne of Green Gables*. Chapter 21. New York: Dover Publications, 2002.

O'Donell, Daniel. Lyrics and music *Only This Moment is Mine*. Original publication Valentine Music Group, Ltd. Recorded live at the Gleneagle Hotel, Killarney, Ireland, *The Daniel O'Donnell Show 2001.* Dublin, Ireland, Rosette Productions Ltd., 2002 disc 2, track 5. Used by permission.

Peck, M. Scott. *Abounding Faith: A Treasury of Wisdom*. Kansas City, MO: Andrews McMeel, 2003.

Wayne Dyer. BrainyQuote.com, Xplore Inc, 2015. http://www.brainyquote.com/quotes/quotes/w/waynedyer384143.html, accessed May 20, 2015.

White, Michael. *C. S. Lewis: Creator of Narnia.* New York: Carrol and Graf Publishers, 2005.

Wordsworth, William. *The Complete Poetical Works*. London: Macmillan Company, 1888 .

Quindlen, Anna. *The New York Times*, sect. A, p. 23. May 4, 1994.

CPSIA information can be obtained at www.ICGtesting.com
Printed in the USA
LVOW03s1132100915

453631LV00002B/3/P